LOOK BACK AND LAUGH

Editor-in-chief: Chris Staros. Designed by Liz Prince & Gilberto Lazcano. Published by Top Shelf Productions, P.O. Box 1282, Marietta GA 30061-1282, U.S.A. Top Shelf Productions is an imprint of IDW Publishing, a division of Idea and Design Works, LLC. Offices: 2765 Truxtun Road, San Diego CA 92106.

Visit our online catalog at www.topshelfcomix.com

ISBN 978-1-60309-434-4 Printed in Korea. 21 20 19 18 1 2 3 4

LOOK BACK AND LAUGH

JOURNAL COMICS BY LIZ PRINCE

Introduction

Hello, and welcome to this collection of my 2016 journal comics.

This project started as a way to break out of a crippling writer's block while also completing a lifetime goal of drawing an autobio comic every dang day for a year. These comics were originally produced as patreon exclusive content.

As of this publication in 2018, I am STILL keeping up the daily comic practice! You can follow along at: patreon.com/lizprince

Thanks for reading! Enjoy!

PUNK

JANUARY
2:17

January 2016

Somerville, MA, U.S.A., EARTH

January 1, 2016
I treated Kyle to Indian buffet for lunch.
I've got it.
oh, thank you.
Just keep bringin' that sweet ass.
Ha ha

January 2, 2016

January 3, 2016

I didn't leave the house today except for when I took out the trash.

updating my website

Watching Simpsons DVDs.

Reading The Cuckoo's Calling.

It was a pretty good day.

January 4, 2016

Today was the coldest day of winter so far; only 24 degrees and lightly snowing. I walked to my afternoon appointments in my favorite weather.

January 5, 2016

I've had insomnia for almost 4 months.

Having to be awake all night thinking about myself

It's too much Liz, even for Liz.

January 6, 2016

Had lunch with Eleni, after which we got STICKY BUN MILKSHAKES (vanilla custard, sticky bun goo, and sugared pecans all blended together).

It's January and I'm outside! with a milkshake!

slurp

Then I recorded a podcast with Kevin Budnik over Skype.

Haha, wolfman's looking right at me!

January 7, 2016

11:54 am

Hi Elizabeth, I'll check you in.

Thanks

12:20pm

Sorry, I know your appointment was at 12, but we're running late.

Ok.

12:42pm

Hey, I'm sorry, but can I reschedule? I should have been done by now.

I apologize. Can you come Tuesday?

But on the plus side, I don't have to get my tooth drilled until next week now...

DENTAL

January 8, 2016

On an overnight visit to Portland, ME, Kyle and I:

got free donuts at Holy Donut

went VHS shopping

CRITTERS 4

SNAKE ISLAND

visited an awesome sock store

played pinball and got dinner with

REPLAY

Megan & Danny

and slept in a king size bed.

January 9, 2016

yawn

!

psst, Kyle, it's SNOWING!

groan

January 10, 2016

Ten years ago today, my friend Chris killed himself.

I'm trying to think of something to say about it, but

tap tap

everything sounds dumb.

January 11, 2016

* it actually turned out to be puke.

January 12, 2016

I got soaked walking in an intense, but short-lived snow squall.

So I polished off the evening with waffles and hot chocolate.

And sitting front of the fake fireplace with Wolfman.

Winter is cozy as fuck.

January 13, 2016

Do you want to see The Revenant at 4:15?

Hm, how long is it?

2 hours.

OK, yeah, I have band practice at 7:30, but I'll have enough time.

After the very long movie...

Whoa, it's 6:45! That movie was 2½ hours!

Oops. I guess it said 156 minutes, not 1 hour and 56 minutes. Sorry.

January 14, 2016

My therapist and I are working on helping me practice good self care. The tricky thing is that what self care means can change on a regular basis.

January 15, 2016

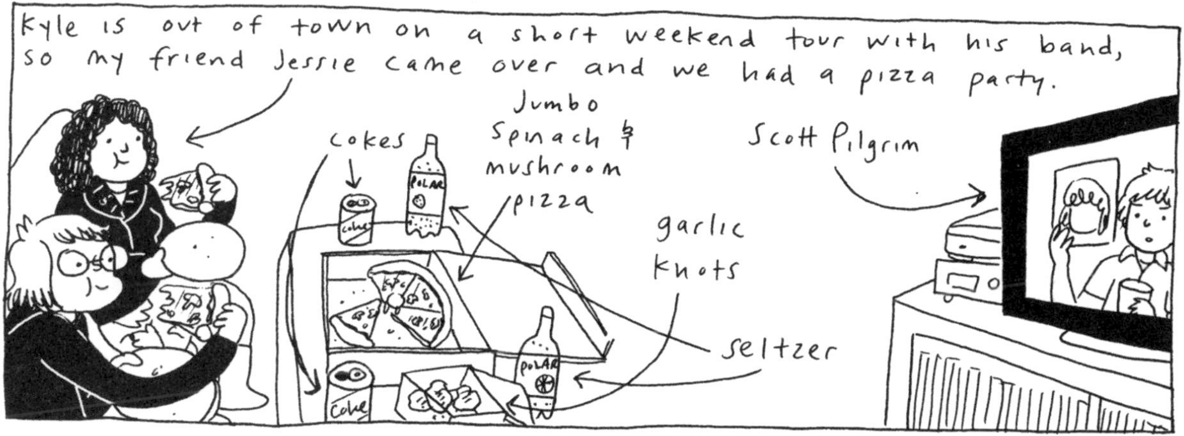

Kyle is out of town on a short weekend tour with his band, so my friend Jessie came over and we had a pizza party.

cokes

Jumbo Spinach & mushroom pizza

Scott Pilgrim

garlic knots

seltzer

January 16, 2016

Today I made soup while across the country my best friend gave birth to her first child.

chop
chop
chop

She made a human while I made dinner.

STIR
STIR

It was a damn good soup, though.

SLURP

January 17, 2016

I bet from reading these comics you'd assume I'm obsessed with eating.

AND IT'S TRUE!

Today I went to Grasshopper vegan buffet with Tim, Eleni, and their 7-month-old baby who didn't care about me.

You should at least be impressed by how much I ate!

Nah.

She's not buyin' it.

January 18, 2016

Wolfman will sit for hours and watch Kyle play video games on his laptop.

January 19, 2016

I was angry, but I had no reason to be.

What's the matter?

Nothing. Everything.

I went to bed early because I got a migraine.

9:41

Now I'm mad because I have a headache.

9:42

Thanks, migraine!

January 20, 2016

♫ Because your kiss, your kiss, ♫

?

UNZIP

♫ IS ON MY LIST ♫

FWUMP

♫ BECAUSE YOUR KISS IS ON MY LIST ♫

FLING

Some time later...

Haha, you got seduced by a Hall & Oates Song!

Finally!

January 21, 2016

ugh, why is this bottle so hard to open?

whoops!

splash

Heh, Will you still love me if I wet my pants during a live interview?

HA HA HA HA HA HA

January 22, 2016

Excuse me, are you Liz Prince?

...Yes?

Oh, wow, this is so cool! I knew you lived here, but I just moved to the area.

Anyway, I don't want to be weird, but I wanted to tell you I'm excited about your patreon!

Ego boost: achieved.

January 23, 2016

Although Boston didn't get much snow, Kyle & I went into blizzard mode.

made enchiladas

Watched the Masterchef Junior semi-finals

And the winner is ADDISON.

YES!*

played Goldeneye
It's kind of upsetting how much of this game I remember.
seltz

*finally the 2 finalists are girls: a girl is going to win for the first time ever!

January 24, 2016

Catching up with Jordyn after she's been out of town for a month:

Check out this hilarious picture of Wolfman!

Ha, was that taken today?

Nah, I just wear the same thing everyday.

January 20,

I had a moment of panic about my patreon today.

Ah! People are actually pledging! Now I have to draw a comic everyday for a whole year!

I calmed down, took a nap, and got vegan cheesesteaks with Razorcake folks.

I only have this little piece of bread left.

Megan, eat all your carbs, young lady!

January 26, 2016

In an effort to fix Dracula's anxiety we put a thundershirt on him

January 27, 2016

What are you doing?

Giving myself a hug.

January 28, 2016

January 29, 2016

I haven't really cared about sports since middle school,

And the next Masterchef JR. is...

so I can't say for sure,

...

but the stress and anticipation I felt watching the Masterchef Junior finale,

...

is probably how people feel about the Superbowl.

ADDISON!

TOUCHDOWN!

January 30, 2016

Kyle was in a bad mood today. He's normally not a very moody person.

Are you mad?

It's a healthy reminder that he's a human who has good days and bad days.

I'm just really stressed out.

January 31, 2016

It was so warm out that I rode to and from work without a jacket or gloves.

Freakish

The Trader Joe's version of Swedish Fish are really good.

"Scandanavian Swimmers"!

Ha!

5 FT

FEBRUARY

February 2016
Somerville, MA, U.S.A., EARTH

February 1, 2016

Kyle and I got Indian buffet...

Hey, we got Indian buffet on the 1st of last month, too!

Then took a walk.

When we get home we should take a little nap, maybe have some sex...

You read my mind!

B

Today was great.

4:15

February 2, 2016

My therapist said: "Isn't the point to experience both the times when drawing is easy and when it's hard? To reaquaint yourself with overcoming the difficulty?"

So well put.

February 3, 2016

At 4:30am when I couldn't sleep, wolfman straddled my arm and sat down.

She then bent her body in half so that I could scratch her chin with my index finger

PURRRR

February 4, 2016

we just happened to do our weekly grocery shopping at the same time as everyone prepping for our weekend snowstorm (also the Superbowl, I guess?).

But there was a deal where if you buy 2 bags of chips you get a FREE salsa!

We got 4 chips!

And 2 salsas!

TOSTITOS

TOSTITOS

All for only $8!

February 5, 2016

So much awesome stuff happened today I can hardly cram it all into one comic.

It snowed big heavy flakes all day and I took an hour long walk.

Then I forced Kyle outside to view the spectacular pink-yellow sunset on the snow-covered trees.

Isn't it AMAZING?

I guess. I'm cold.

And the best part: Nicole got stuck in Boston on her way home from Paris and she stayed at my house!

You're here!

I'm here!

February 6, 2016

Hey, does asparagus just grow out of the ground as single stalks?

Yeah, see?

gasp They look like LAND EELS!

February 7, 2016

Today I used a photocopier to make a comic book for the first time in 6 years.

Historically I have experienced a lot of set backs when using a copy machine, so it's a stressful process!

Turned out I was worried for no reason (as usual). There wasn't a single paper jam or misprinted page.

February 8, 2016

TIME TO ASSEMBLE THESE COMICS!

FOLD

JANUARY

STAPLE

JANUARY

JANUARY

TRIM

STAMP

THANKS TO

STUFF

ADDRESS

LICK

ew

REPEAT x 74!

February 9, 2016

February 10, 2016

Today I got lunch with Eleni and we had BEET SODAS.

wow, beet soda. who knew?

February 11, 2016

Hi, can I get a 'shroom burger and cheese fries?

wow, that's a lot of cheese.

You don't know me.

February 12, 2016

Jordyn, Kyle and I played Super Mario 2 while we awaited our food delivery.

I only play as the Princess.

Really? I'm all about Luigi.

I like Toad.

Does anyone ever play as Mario?

What would be the point? He has no special power.

B

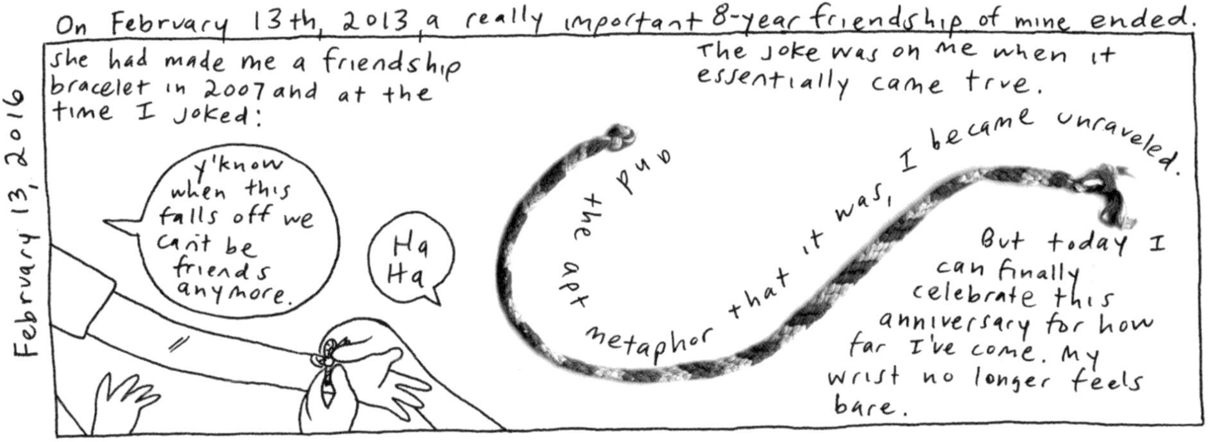

February 13, 2016

On February 13th, 2013, a really important 8-year friendship of mine ended.

She had made me a friendship bracelet in 2007 and at the time I joked:

Y'know when this falls off we can't be friends anymore.

Ha Ha

The joke was on me when it essentially came true.

And the apt metaphor that it was, I became unraveled.

But today I can finally celebrate this anniversary for how far I've come. My wrist no longer feels bare.

February 14, 2016

you should write your comics BEFORE they happen, and then make them come true.

Oh, like, "Today Kyle bought me dinner."?

And then you'd have to buy me dinner! Or "Today Kyle cleaned the entire kitchen." OOOOHH.

How about "Today Kyle took a shower"!!

ok! I get it.

SUGARFREAK

February 15, 2016

I've been trying to eat less sugar because my dentist advised it.

But we got a lot of candy at xmas.

it would be fucked not to eat this box of fancy chocolates.

And there were these new Oreos I had to try...

If I don't support this, who will?

Filled Cupcake OREO

Then Kyle got me a quintessential Valentine's gift.

Cute!

LIZ

And I might've bought myself 2 bags of Scandinavian Swimmers...

I have a problem.

SCANDINAVIAN SWIMMERS

February 16, 2016

What's that bump on your chin?

PURRRRRRRR

AH! It's a big scab!

Hey!

Oh no! What if Wolfman has CAT ACNE?!

So? You have human acne and you're 34.

February 17, 2016

February 18, 2016

I look my best as a reflection in the subway window when it's underground. Not enough detail to betray my awkward teenage complexion: just a vague hint of my features.

I guess I look how I draw myself.

Cranston, RI

Kyle and I went to Providence to stay with my brother's family for the night.

We stopped at some thrift stores on the way down, where I scored

a vampire candle holder

NO BODY HERE

a cool soccer scarf

February 20, 2016
Cranston, RI
8:30 AM
YAP!
LEAP
BARK BARK
How did the dogs get in here!
ugh!
slobber
BARK BARK BARK
Did you release the hounds on us?
Yep. Good morning.
NAMASTE HOME WITH MY DOG.

February 21, 2016
Palm City, FL

After a 3½-hour flight, Kyle and I are in South Florida with his dad.

I'm gonna open it halfway, then you look up.

GASP

TREE FROGS!

February 22, 2016

I've never been good at relaxing, but I think I'm doing well on this trip.

February 23, 2016
Palm City, FL

February 24, 2016
Palm City, FL

Went fishing on a boat with a dog.

Not my brother's frenchie, but a pretty eerie doppelganger named Duncan!

Nobody caught any fish but I had the honor of catching the biggest stick.

Then torrential rainstorms ripped through the area.

Yikes!

My first time wearing a hoodie in 2 days!

February 25, 2016
Palm City, FL
Took advantage of the sun before flying back to Boston.
3FT
I'll miss the frogs and the fun, but I was excited to get home to Wolfman & Dracula.
I missed you so much.
PURRRRR
PURRRRR
And it turns out that I took home a sunburn as a souvenir.
Ack! what an amateur!

February 26, 2016

February 27, 2016

Was social and went out to vegan brunch with some people I haven't really hung out with much before.

Not freaking out.

Then I hung out with the people I hang out with everyday.

Still not freaking out.

February 28, 2016
Hey. So, I can't do it.
I can't keep drawing myself with this haircut.
There are lots of things about my caricature that are inaccurate.
For instance, my glasses are square, and my nose is big.
And I have a lot of tattoos that I don't draw myself with.*
*because they end up looking like a skin rash.
Yeah, so take a hike! This Liz is bettr.
HEY!
SHOVE

February 29, 2016

Kyle and I share an office and my desk is always too cluttered to work at.

fish stapler

jar of pens

sketchbooks and bristol pads

wolfman looking out the window

magazines and library books

daily planner

bin of art supplies

coaster

bin of paper

mail

My fantasies have become overwhelmingly non-sexual.

A room of my own. mmmm.

MARCH
B

March 2016

Somerville, MA, U.S.A., Earth

March 1, 2016

Kyle and I voted and continued our tradition of Indian buffet on the 1st of the month.

SHOVEL

CHOMP

I needed a nap because I still haven't been sleeping well.

3:17

I awoke with a general sense of malaise.

Maybe I just won't get out of bed.

works for me.

March 2, 2016

While brushing Dracula's teeth I discovered that he also has cat acne.

Not you too!

Cat acne isn't especially dangerous if you keep it under control.

Washing their bowls nightly

But do yourself a favor and DO NOT google image search it.

That'd better not happen to my cats!

March 3, 2016
Book making day 1

I carried a ream of cardstock and 2 reams of legal size paper to make photocopies.

And here I thought being hunched over drawing would be the cause of my back problems.

on the T a guy in sweat-pants farted on my head.
BRAP

After cutting & folding covers I realized that the ink on my metallic purple cardstock smudges.
And here I thought that guy farting on me would be the worst thing that happened to me today.

March 4, 2016
Book Making Day 2

I had to handle my books very carefully to avoid the ink on the covers.

Must... not... smudge.

Folding books w/ wax paper

And not only was the smudging a problem, but the cover stock was so thick that I had to trim the interior pages separately.

TWICE the work.

None of the fun.

As a reward for my hard work, Kyle and I went to Ocean State Job Lot* to blow off some steam.

SO MANY JARS OF DISCOUNT MUSTARD!

SPICY

*a discount store akin to BIG LOTS.

March 5, 2016
Book Making Day 3

I just couldn't catch a break on this book. Today while packing envelopes I spilled the water I was using to wet the envelope glue.

Whoever has my voodoo doll needs to STOP.

March 6, 2016

HA HA HA

?

HAHAHA

BONK!

Sorry, it's funny! She's been head-butting you a long time!

PURRR

Richmond, VA

I flew to Richmond today to spend a few days with Nicole.*

I really like the houses here.

Cute!

* see February 5th's comic!

March 8, 2016
Richmond, VA

For International Women's Day Nicole wore the most appropriate shirt.

FUCK YOU

We went thrifting.

Should I get this shirt?

Yes. Should I get these leggings.

Yes.*

BASEBALL CAMP

*she didn't.

And we went to GWAR bar - a theme bar owned by the shock metal band GWAR.

Let's get the seitan wings.*

But let's not get "Bowel Corrupter" sauce.

MENU

GWAR

*they are called "wangs" on the menu, but fuck that.

March 9, 2016
Richmond, VA

On my last morning in Richmond I felt like I was getting in the way. It wasn't anything Nicole did

I need some quiet work time.

OK

I have huge issues with feeling like an inconvenience because my Dad treated me like one for most of my teen years.

AAHCHOO!

UGH I need quiet!

It's good to have a language to deal with these feelings now.

This feeling is just a projection of how you're used to being treated. It's not here now.

March 10, 2016

For me the hardest part of writing these comics is having to chose what to highlight on the days that are entertaining.

Watching a giant tree get lifted piece-by-piece with a hydraulic lift

Delicious vegan tacos

Fetch with Ponyo

Hilarious/uplifting conversations with Nicole

And having to fill the space on the days that are not.

March 11, 2016

Kyle & I are thrifty shoppers with a seltzer habit: we always get two 12 packs of whatever's on sale.

4 for $10 this week

But today there was a new seltzer we decided to try even though it was $4.99 for a 4 pack!

*actually, I don't really sleep at night anyway.

March 12, 2016

Lately everything takes longer than I think it will.

what the heck! How is it 11:30 already?!

JK, I don't wear a watch.

There are so many things I've been putting on the back-burner (for, like, my whole life)

Hmm

YOUR LIFE

1 BUSY 2 BUSY 3 BUSY 4 due date 5 BUSY 6 BUSY
7 BUSY 8 BUSY 9 BUSY 10 BUSY 11 OU 12 T O 13 F —
14 TOWN 15 16 17 18 19 20 BUSY
21 work 22 BUSY 23 BUSY 24 work 25 BUSY 26 BUSY 27 BUSY
28 work 29 BUSY 30 BUSY 13 work

Maybe I'll have time in 2018...

Thusly,

Stupid Daylight Savings! I don't have time to lose an hour.

March 13, 2016

I am feeling frazzled. My sleeping problems have been bad this week, and waking up with one less hour today made me extra sluggish.

I'm going to Macedonia on Wednesday to teach a series of comics workshops for the U.S. Embassy, and although I've known about this trip for 6 months, I've put off planning until today.

So why are you still procrastinating!?!?

But I'm so close to beating this Candy Blast level.

March 14, 2016

Today was a perfect day for staying home in my PJs getting shit DONE.

Update my workshop for Macedonia ✓

That'll learn 'em.

Catch up on my projects ✓

Another one bites the dust ♫

Convince Kyle to walk to the store in the rain to get me an ice cream sandwich ✓

You DO love me!

Maybe a little.

March 15, 2016

I don't want to go to Macedonia. I want to stay home with Wolfman.*

?

*Because I'm a homebody who is afraid to fly.

But look at all the awesome food we can eat there!

Tavre Gravce

Shopska Salad

Yeah... but still, Wolfman!

You're GOING somewhere!?

March 16, 2016
This morning Wolfman refused to look at me.
I'm gonna miss you SO MUCH, wolfman.
Then don't go, you jerk.
we had to fly to Washington DC, then backtrack east to fly across the Atlantic Ocean on the most turbulent flight I've ever been on.
SHAKE
BOUNCE
what if that's the last time I see wolfman, and she was mad at me!?

March 11, 2016
Skopje, Macedonia

Wednesday bled into Thursday as we crossed many time zones, landed in Vienna, and then flew to Skopje. After a much-needed nap at our hotel my embassy hosts took Kyle and I to a traditional Macedonian restaurant housed in a building from the 1500s Ottoman Empire.

This was a hotel during the Ottoman times! You can still see the posts where travelers tied up their camels.

March 18, 2016
Skopje, Macedonia

Skopje is a city with many new monuments made to look old.

That fountain was built in 2014, and many locals dis-like it. It looks like Las Vegas.

I can see that.

Amid some truly old buildings that survived a devastating earthquake in 1963.

Kale Fortress
c. 550 A.D.

It can be hard to tell the difference between the authentic and the in-authentic as a tourist.

Which magnet should we get?!

SKOPJE

March

Krusevo, Macedonia

Today I traveled to Krusevo, a town high up in the Balkan mountains.

On the way there our van got pulled over and the driver bribed the police not to give him a ticket.

It is unfortunately very common here.

I did a workshop with the students who read Tomboy as part of their graphic novel class.

Draw a picture for me!

Me, too!

I want one!

Draw one for me!

March 20, 2016
Krusevo, Macedonia

Being an introverted person traveling in a foreign country, meeting so many new people and seeing so many new places can be taxing. Even when you're enjoying yourself.

I returned to the hotel in Skopje and tried to relax and reset.

March
Skopje, Macedonia

The highlight of my day was meeting an amazing group of elementary school kids in a small village next to an oil refinery 30km outside of Skopje.

March 22, 2016
Skopje, Macedonia

After a week of doing the same presentation about my work 3 times a day, I'm pretty tired of talking about myself.

Blah Blah Blah

Kill me.

TOMBOY

This is the last day of my visit to Macedonia.

Did you ever think comics would bring you <u>here</u>?

Watching bats from my hotel balcony ↘

Zurich, Switzerland

places we slept* during our 8 hour layover at the Zurich airport:

A set of seats.

A booth at an airport restaurant.

A different set of seats.

* for less than an hour at a time.

March 24, 2016

coming home from a trip is a mixed blessing. A comforting reality check.

We were only gone for a week! The amount of cat hair all over everything makes it look like we were gone for a year!

VROOOOM

I'm glad you can enjoy the 2 loads of laundry I've done today.

PURRRR

One of the cats threw up while you were brushing your teeth.

March 25, 2016

While I was in Macedonia Polar released a limited edition April Fool's Day Seltzer.

POLAR
SELTZER
UNICORN
KISSES

UNICORN KISSES!!!!!

NEED!

People were saying it's hard to find, so when I got back I immediately began my search.

Aw, they don't have it.

Will you make fun of me if I cry because I can't find the Unicorn flavor seltzer?

Mercilessly.

B

March 26, 2016

GLEE

POLAR
SELTZER
UNICORN
KISSES

March 27, 2016

Dracula's anxiety is getting worse.

It's okay, buddy, I just want to pet you.

ZIP

You're breaking my heart, Drakey.

Can't we just get him the drugs already?

March 28, 2016

I haven't socially left the house since getting home from Macedonia.

I've got cabin fever.

I wonder what outside air tastes like.

But I'm far too stressed out about meeting deadlines before I go to Seattle next week to do anything about it.

Why do you keep kicking air?

March 29, 2016

As I was leaving I ran into my housemate who was unloading books for his comic shop.

Oh! Can I borrow this?

Sure.

PATIENCE

CLOWES

The sun reflected off the foil stamped title, burning my vision so it was all I could see for a ½ hour.

PATIENCE

Later I had dinner with Jordyn.

I just want to thank you for not bringing up the fact that I have a hickey.

Oh man, it was taking all my willpower!

March 30, 2016

I impressed myself with my work ethic today.

Left the house at 2 for my tax appointment.

I just want to apologize in advance for what's about to go down.

envelope bulging with receipts and 1099s.

Then went straight to the library and worked until 9

NB237-ND497

At least at this job the taxes get taken out.

I rode my bike home and stayed up until 1 working on the cover for March's book.

The old Liz would have said "fuck it" and gone to bed by now.

I miss the old Liz.

March 31, 2016

My therapist dropped some wisdom on me during our session.

I think people tend to find happiness more readily if they realize that a lot of the situations they're in come from choices they made.

So I chose to spend my evening talking with a 9-month-old.

glabble ga!

She's never been this vocal before!

blabbidy blah!

DABA!

APRIL

April, 2016

Somerville, MA, U.S.A., Earth

April 1, 2016

Tim and El joined us for our monthly Indian buffet date.

OMG! They have mutter paneer!

What's that?

PEAS AND CHEESE!

I ate so much that I didn't even really want to eat dinner.

Should we make something?

What's the point? It won't be as good as lunch.

April 2, 2016

Being in Europe reset my sleeping schedule, so for the first time in 6 or 7 months I've been reliably sleeping through the night.

Z

April 3, 2016

I went to a private room karaoke place with Mike, Lauren, and Jordyn.

I'LL MAKE LOVE TO YOU

LIKE YOU WANT ME TO

AND I WILL NOT LET GO TIL YOU TELL ME TO

YOUR SCORE 22/100

POOR!

you could at least give me points for enthusiasm...

April 4, 2016
Good morning, I'm gonna open the blinds.
OK
Whoa!
Look at all that SNOW!
groan

April 5, 2016

Few things make me happier than bringing a bunch of mail to the post office.

TAMPED
ETTERS

STAMP
LETTE

April 6, 2016
Seattle, WA

Wolfman tried a new tactic to keep me from going on my trip.

You've gotta get past me first!

* But only slightly

April 7, 2016
Emerald City Comicon day 1

I felt like I might have a panic attack and the con hadn't even started yet.

I left my xanax in the hotel...

April 8, 2016
Emerald City Comicon day 2

So, did you go out and party last night? Get drunk at the hotel bar with other cartoonists?

LIZ PRINCE 2-08

PETER BAGGE 2-09

Well, I partied the Liz Prince way, which means I got takeout from the Cheesecake Factory, ate it in bed, and was asleep by 9:30.

LIZ PRINCE 2-08

PETER BAGGE 2-09

Jeez, that's the saddest thing I've ever heard.

Really? I feel like it definitely ranks in the top 5 nights of my life.

LIZ PRINCE 2-08

PETER BAGGE 2-09

April 9, 2016
Emerald City Comicon day 3

I woke up with a headache, but had a really good time being on a YA books panel first thing in the morning.

Royden Lepp
Hope Larson
me (duh)
Raina Telgemeier (as Ponyo)
Faith Erin Hicks
Sierra Hahn

But then I went full-on migraine for the rest of the day.

Thank god this is my last day of these comic con shenanigans.

April 10, 2016
Trailer Blaze day 1

I used $15 in "Green Choice"* vouchers to get room service breakfast and still had to pay $15!

This is NOT a $30 breakfast. This is bullshit.

Hate-eating an omelet.

I skipped the last day of Emerald City Comicon to go to an all women's comics residency at the Sou'wester in Seaview, Washington. For the next 5 days an old trailer will be my studio.

This is MUCH more my speed.

* A hotel program that gives you food vouchers if you opt out of daily linen service.

April 11, 2016
Trailer Blaze day 2

I took advantage of the only sunny day in the forecast for this week.

Walked to the laundromat

So mesmerizing.

Visited Jake the Alligator Man.

Hiya Jake!

Hey Liz!

Ate an obnoxious amount of salt water taffy on my walk back to the Sou'wester.

April 12, 2016
Trailer Blaze day 3

It was stormy all day, and at times the sound of the raindrops pelting the metal roof of my trailer was deafening. I do this thing where I have difficult conversations with people in my head. It's a coping method for both before and after a confrontation, which allows me to have control over the outcome, or prepare myself for the direction an impending situation might take, by allowing myself to dictate the reactions of both parties.

For a trailer with only one occupant, it was an awfully noisy day.

April 13 2016
Trailer Blaze day 4

I needed to ensure that I didn't repeat yesterday's emotional turbulence, so I took a long afternoon walk on the beach.

Jessica and I cooked the group meal for the residency in my tiny trailer kitchen.

Cooking chili in a thin pot with uneven heat

This feels kind of like we're on Cutthroat Kitchen.

Sawing limes with a warped, dull knife

BLACK BEANS

April 14, 2016
Trailer Blaze day 5

Kettner & Lacy drove up from Portland for the day to see the WA coast landmarks.

I wanna touch it, too.

GREY WHALE SKELETON

poke

THE GIANT FRY PAN

LONG BEACH WASH

WATER-SQUIRTING RAZOR CLAM SCULPTURE

Meh.

I like it!

April 15, 2016
Tacoma, WA

This morning I said goodbye to the Trailer Blaze group and headed up to Tacoma to stay with my friends Dana & Jon.

JANELLE
SARAH
KELLY
EROYN
MEGAN
GILLIAN
EMILIE
JESSICA
ROBYN
MITA

It was Jon's birthday, and thusly we celebrated:

Wow, I really jumped off the deep end after my 5 years of not drinking.

SCORPION BOWL
JELLO SHOTS

April 16, 2016
Tacoma, WA

Dana & Jon hosted a BBQ in their new backyard for Jon's birthday. Being around a lot of new people for an extended period of time very quickly depletes my social resources.

Z

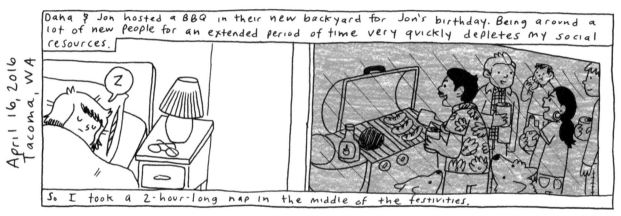

So I took a 2-hour-long nap in the middle of the festivities.

April 11, 2010
Tacoma, WA

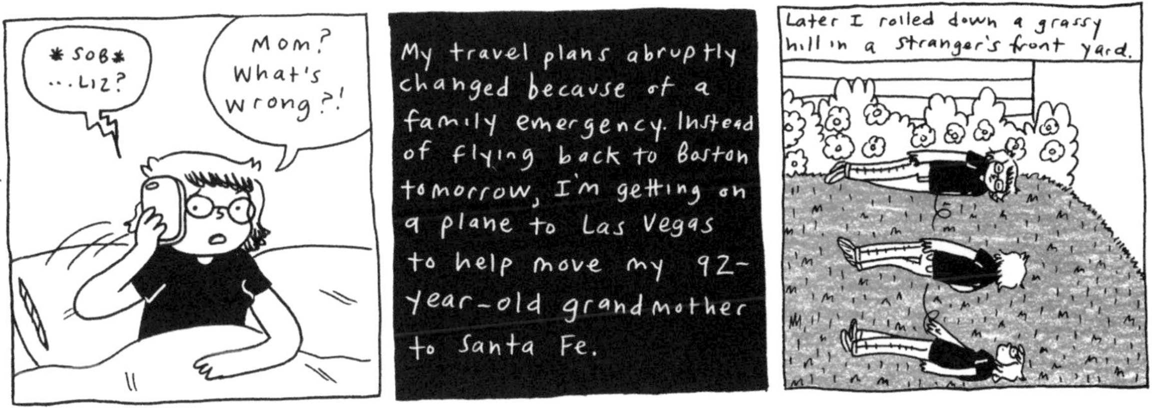

SOB ...LIZ?

Mom? What's wrong?!

My travel plans abruptly changed because of a family emergency. Instead of flying back to Boston tomorrow, I'm getting on a plane to Las Vegas to help move my 92-year-old grandmother to Santa Fe.

Later I rolled down a grassy hill in a stranger's front yard.

April 18, 2016
Las Vegas, NV
I wonder if the person viewing this x-ray can tell I have a really bad wedgie right now.
That woman's foot is in my space.
I hate flying.
Thank you for coming to help me, Lizzy.
I'd do it again in a heartbeat, my mommy.

April 19, 2016
Las Vegas, NV

My grandma has lived with my aunt for 25 years, but my aunt is in the hospital, and when she gets out it's doubtful she'll be able to continue to be her mom's caregiver.

Why did this happen to... oh! I keep forgetting my daughter's name. The one that's in the hospital?

Why can't I ever remember her name?

Besides memory issues that get worse by the day, my grandma needs someone to help her with hygiene, take care of household chores and decipher her bills and write her checks.

Did you get the mail? Do I have any bills? Did you add them to my balance book?

Did the mail come? Did you write my checks in the balance book?

But despite all of this, she's extremely angry that we want to take her to Santa Fe to care for her.

This is a conspiracy! You planned it! You made her go to the hospital so you can take my money and dump me on the street!

I'm not going! I'D RATHER DIE!

Stick a knife in my back!

April 20, 2016
Santa Fe, NM

I was awake all night worrying about what it will be like to get grandma on the plane.

Shockingly she did a complete 180 emotional ollie.

Are you OK, Grandma?

... yes. I'm happy.

April 21, 2016
Santa Fe, NM

My mom's house is very different from the house my grandma lived in in Vegas.

How come there's no TV in the bedroom? I can't sleep without a TV.

Sorry, you'll have to get used to it.

Do you have any soda?

No.

Grandma keeps getting lost in the hallway,

LINDA! I can't find the bathroom!

and forgetting where we put her things.

HELP!

I can't find my panties!

April 22, 2016
Santa Fe, NM

I dropped my mom off for a much-needed massage and did some shopping for my grandma's essentials.

I hope these are the right ones.

I felt bad having to leave my mom so soon during this difficult time, but I've been out of town for 3 weeks at this point and I'm falling behind on LIFE.

I love you, mom.

I don't know what I would have done with-out you.

The silver lining of this impromptu trip to Santa Fe was getting to stay with Alec & Claire and meeting my goddaughter, Suzanne.

She already dislikes me. Smart kid!

WAH

April 23, 2016

Thank you for holding, how may I help you?

Yes, hello. I'm on the Santa Fe to Denver flight that keeps getting delayed due to mechanical failure. At this point I've missed both my original connection to Boston, and the one I was re-booked on. I see online that there's a seat on a non-stop flight that leaves Denver at 5:52pm and gets into Boston at 11:45pm; can I please be booked on that flight?

Oh, no, I'm sorry, ma'am, but that seat is a first-class ticket, and we can't give that to a coach passenger.

Ok, so lemme get this straight...

You're saying that even though this delay is the airlines' fault, and my original Boston flight was non-stop, you're going to make me fly to Chicago, then Boston, getting in at 1am, instead of putting me on a direct flight because I'm not wealthy?

... Yes.

Well, fuck you very much, United Airlines.

April 24, 2016

wow, I really love this guy.

April 25, 2016

I was supposed to have jury duty this morning, but when my alarm went off at 6am I decided to say FUCK IT.

RING -A- DING RING -A- DI~

Nope.

I thought I was gonna be in trouble, but:

Oh, that's fine, sweetheart, don't worry about it. But our computer system is down today, so can you call back later to re-schedule?

Sure, thanks!

So I was free to do whatever I wanted with the rest of my day.

I don't want you to get a regular job again: we won't have afternoon sex anymore.

It has done wonders for our sex life.

Moral: I'm a degenerate.

April 26, 2016

At the post office

Hey Liz, are you getting married?

Um, no? Does something in my mail make it seem like I am?

No, but my niece just got engaged and she's 30, so since you're older I thought maybe you were thinking of getting married, too.

I see, well, I firmly believe that age ain't nothin' but a number, and that marriage is strictly for tax purposes.

April 27, 2016

Kyle and I brought back some ajvar* from Skopje

MAMA'S
HOMESTYLE
AJVAR

+

and we recently discovered that the grocery store sells discounted random cheese pieces

DELI SPECIAL CHEESE ENDS

+

so if I just add some cucumber

=

I can replicate what I ate for breakfast every morning in Macedonia!

ZANG

* a spread made from roasted red peppers and eggplant

April 28, 2016

April 29, 2016

BRUSH
BRUSH
BRUSH
PURRRRRRRR

April 30, 2016

Today I got an ego boost by being recognized in the bathroom at work.

OH MY GOD! What are you doing here? I'm YOUR BIGGEST fan!

Later on Kyle, Tim, El and I saw Keanu at the theater with the crazy armchair stadium seats.

B

MAY

May 2016

Somerville, MA, U.S.A., Earth

May 1, 2016

Another month, another Indian buffet.

gasp They have peas & cheese! That's twice in a row!

MUTTER

May 2, 2016

I re-read my comics from January, and it was eye-opening to see the evolution of the content and the quality of art.

JANUARY

Both can, at least partially, be attributed to my "Zoloft" prescription.

These magic pills have allowed me to worry less and create more.

Tiny, but powerful.

I'm very fortunate that the first medication I tried worked for me. I know that a lot of people have to try several medicines, or combinations thereof, before they find something that helps.

#blessed.

May 3, 2016

I'm reading a book that is depressing as fuck. Sometimes it makes me nauseous, sometimes it makes me cry.

But while the cover image is very striking, I can't stop obsessing over how this image contradicts the theme of the book. A sun-bleached wall with the photos missing indicates that the same family has lived there a long time.

EVICTED
EVICTED
POVERTY AND PROFIT IN THE AMERICAN CITY
MATTHEW DESMOND

This is a book about families that get evicted a few times a year.

May 4, 2016

OW WOLFMAN!

You can't just jump on my back when I'm standing up! Your claws hurt!

May 5, 2016

This morning I worked, then Kyle and I did yoga. When I got out of the shower I had a voicemail.

Hi Liz, it's after 11 and I'm wondering where you are. I hope you're ok. Call me back when you can.

I had somehow completely forgotten about therapy.

I'm so sorry, I don't know what happened. In my mind Thursday was my day this week that I could just work on my projects with no other obligations but that doesn't make sense because we always meet on Thursdays.

It's fine, these things happen. I'm just glad everything is ok. You can give yourself a break on this one.

...If only it were that easy!

May 6, 2016

Kyle took me on a surprise trip to the Museum of Science to see the Frogs: A Chorus of Colors exhibit for our 4th anniversary.

May 7, 2016

Hey mom, I have something to tell you: Kyle and I are getting MARRIED.

Oh, honey, that's wonderful!

Wait... you're not taking his last name, are you?

NO! Are you fucking CRAZY?!

Good.

May 8, 2016

I slept on the couch because I was writhing in pain with horrible cramps.

May 9, 2016

At the library the student employee used me for a class project.

I have to write an obituary for an artist I like, can I write about you?

FINALLY.

Kyle picked me up after work.

I peed out of my butt twice tonight.

Why would you tell me that?

We went to Harvard Sq. to pick up my cut comic pages, and ended up at Tasty Burger.

...Maybe this isn't the best idea right now.

May 10, 2016

Kyle's mom came over and we told her about our engagement.

I'm crying! I'm just so happy!

oops. Everyone seems more excited than Kyle & I are.

She also brought us 23 bottles of the Cinco de Mayo Polar Seltzer flavor, Jalapeno Citrus margarita.

¡Dios mio!

Where are we gonna put these?!

May 11, 2016

Gotta finish my Garfield comic

Gotta send patreon books

me

you

Gotta catch up on my daily comics

Gotta stop thinking about all this shit so I can get some damn sleep!

May 12, 2016

After a week of cold rain, the sun finally came out.
wearing shorts for the first time* this season!

*in Boston.

Kyle and I met up with Kurt and Jane at Taco Party, then brought food back to our house to eat in the back yard.
when I was out here earlier today, a bird POOPED on me!
...oh, good...
well, odds are it won't happen again.
TOSTITOS

Nothing like driving into the woods on a foggy FRIDAY THE 13TH.

May 14, 2016
Bowdoin, ME

Today a cow screamed in my face.

MOOOOOOOO

We had a cookout at Reuben and Tessa's farm.

Who was the host of America's Most Wanted?

John Walsh.

Did he host Unexplained Mysteries too?

No, that was Robert Stack.

And Kyle finally got to hold a snake.

Don't put it in my face!

May 15, 2016
I hated that house.
I agree.

That house needed a lot of work, but I liked it.
NO.

I thought that one was pretty nice...
Ew, not my style AT ALL.

I love it!

May 16, 2016

I wish there was a pause button I could hit when too many things happen at once.

PUSH TO STOP THE WORLD

Instead I've been taking a lot of stress naps.

You're just wasting time.

Maybe if you'd shut up I could get enough rest to get some real work done.

I think you should BOTH shut up.

May 17, 2016

Getting Dracula's blood tested to see if he can start taking Prozac...

So, this must be "Dracula". Can I call him Vlad?

Um, he doesn't respond to that.

Oh, but, haha, get it? Vlad the Impaler: Dracula?

...yes.

You could've just laughed at the joke.

He's my cat. I'll decide what's funny.

May 18, 2016

Getting Dracula's blood tested to see if he can start taking Prozac...

Kyle and I took a class on making an offer on a home tonight.

Note to self: CAPITALISM IS FUCKED.

Then we walked home and discussed the future,

What if we bought something that needed a lot of work, but was cheap.

That could be cool.

and everything seems full of possibilities.

May 19, 2016

I was suffering from a pretty serious case of spring fever so I dicked around today.

Got pizza with Eleni

This potato pizza RULES

Yeah, it's one of my faves.

Jessie introduced me to the magic of set price fro-yo.

put more toppings on!

If you insist.

Then I saw Green Room with Kyle.

Jesus!

Ha ha, ew.

May 20, 2016

My insomnia seems to have returned.

Hey DING-DONG, nightime is for SLEEPING.

I got up early so I could get to work by 9.

BEEP BEEP BEEP

7:30

Don't bother waking me up. I never really went to sleep.

May 21, 2016

I'm here to pick up a prescription for my cat, Dracula.
Yes, is there more than 1 Dracula?
Dracula Prince?
whoa! what about "Wolfman"?
There is.
hmm..
You've got the only "Wolfman".
YES!
But my jubilation subsided when I had a crisis over the moral implications of giving my cat mood medication.
...I don't know how I feel about this...

May 22, 2016

Ended up waiting an hour for a table at brunch with Joel & Jordyn.

Maybe we should just go somewhere else.

But we've waited so long already! It'd be a waste if we left.

On my way home I almost got creamed by an extremely careless driver.

WHOA!

Turning left onto a side street without signaling

The guy angrily shrugged at me, while two teenaged girls looked horrified in the backseat.

So which are you: A shitty dad or a shitty Uber driver?!

May 23, 2016

My bad bike luck continued when I got "pulled over" by a cop for the first time.
Do you know why I pulled you over, miss?
Because I went through a red light.*
Because you're a blowhard who has nothing better to do than harass a bike commuter?
*After coming to a complete stop at an intersection where NO ONE was coming.
Another work day at the library.
uh, just so you know, it's the 23rd, not the 22nd.
Oops.
So you're saying it's painfully obvious that I'm not used to the 9-5 lifestyle?

May 24, 2016

Ok, so I wrap my legs around him so he can't squirm away, pry his mouth open, then squirt the medicine in.

SQUIRT

HACK SPIT

... I take it that's not supposed to happen?

I don't consider that successful. NO.

drool

May 25, 2016

I spent an abnormal amount of time on the phone today

With my mom:

I don't know what to do. Your grandmother is driving me crazy. I'm at my wit's end.

MWWMMM Mom!

I'm in the bathroom! You need to give me a minute to myself!

With my vet: If the liquid isn't working, we can compound the prozac into treats that Dracula might like better...

Yes, I think he would find that preferable to having a syringe forced down his throat.

With my vet's pharmacy:

What's your pet's name?

Dracula Prince.

Prince?

Yeah, like the artist formerly known as. RIP.

OH.

May 26, 2016

Kyle went to Baltimore for Maryland Deathfest, so I had a LIZ night:

ordered Indian food delivery:

INHALE

peas & cheese w/naan

which I ate while watching Jeopardy:

Can no one defeat Buzzy?

And our 9-day returning champion will be back tomorrow.

Then I spent the rest of the night at my drawing desk blasting Taylor Swift:

Now we got bad blood

May 27, 2016
Happy Birthday Kyle!

The library's re-barcoding project started today. It involves scanning the old SMFA barcode,

Beep

confirming that the cataloging record is correct, attaching a new tufts barcode, then scanning that into the system.

I was forewarned that it would be monotonous busy-work that would make my eyes glaze over, but I LOVED IT.

No really, I think it's fun!

Boop

May 28, 2016

I baked* and decorated a cake by myself for the first time.

HAPPY BATDAY KYLE

* A box mix, but still.

May 29, 2016

Everyone had been raving about The Witch, so tonight Kyle & I finally watched it.

I can't understand a thing they're saying.

Me neither.

I'm gonna see if there's subtitles.

Ooh, good idea!

Anyway, once we could tell what was going on I thought it was pretty good.

May 30, 2016

Ew, what's that?

Whoa! Gross! It's a flattened squirrel and its head is covered in MAGGOTS! Come look!
NO!

Aw, but I want us to look at the gross thing TOGETHER.
NO!

May 31, 2016

Today Dracula's tuna flavor Prozac treats came in the mail, as well as some "blanks," which are treats without medicine so we can get him the kind he likes most.

Turns out he likes NONE of them.

JUNE

June 2016

Somerville, MA, U.S.A., Earth

June 1, 2016

How is it JUNE already!? The year is half over! I've got 100 unread emails!!

I haven't even started on projects I thought I'd have COMPLETED by now!!

I get why you're freaked, but I can't breathe.

June 2, 2016

Our Indian buffet date had to happen today because I worked at the library all day on the 1st. Afterwards we got a couples massage.

Talking about buying a house with our mouths full.

Whenever I get a massage I realize that I really just want someone to play with my hair.

...probably wouldn't go over well if I asked...

June 3, 2016
At first when we'd talk about moving, it was more out of necessity than desire,
but the longer I've sat with it, at this point the desire to move trumps the necessity.
So, you're excited about it.
oh, wow, yeah!
I hadn't realized that!

June 4, 2016

Did a workshop at the Boston Children's Book Festival, Hubbub.

LO MY NAME I.

LIZ PRINCE

...this is me on the stage and on the screen at the, same time!

It's a really rewarding experience to inspire kids to write about issues that are important to them.

Thanks for teaching us comics.

We like cats, too!

TOMBOY

June 5, 2016

Buyer signature

Buyer signature

Ok, well, this is exciting! I'll call you when I have news, hopefully very soon!

Thanks

...Did that really just happen?...

June 6, 2016

work was a blessing today: I was too busy to be nervous about our house offer.
Doot-Dee-Doo, Just gotta keep busy.
Boop

But the floodgates opened the second work ended.
why haven't we heard back yet? what if there's another offer?

Also Dracula has figured out how to eat around his prozac treat when I mash it up into real tuna.
Touché, Dracula.
Heh Heh Heh.

June 7, 2016

After a night devoid of sleep due to worry,

We have a counter-offer on our hands.

What should we do?

And a day of low productivity due to fretting...

When will we hear if our counter-counter-offer is accepted?

Maybe I can will the phone to ring.

CONGRATS! You're under contract!

No, congrats to YOU, because you just made our xmas card list!

I went home early and took a long nap with Wolfman.

Z

Z

And successfully tricked Dracula into eating his Prozac by mixing it into wet food.

MWAHAHAHAHAHAHAHAHA

SCARF CHOMP

June 9, 2016

My grandmother was diagnosed with a pretty advanced case of dementia and it was recommended she be placed in assisted living memory care.

The decision to put her in the care of others was hard, but caring for someone who is losing their faculties alone is hard too.

In an ideal scenario my mom would be able to depend on her sister for support while making tough decisions for their mom.

So of course in our reality my aunt and cousin call the cops on my mom for doing the best she can in a difficult situation.

June 10, 2016

Sometimes I don't know how to help.

Sometimes I don't know what to say.

Sometimes I just have to accept the fact that I fall short and that that's ok.

June 11, 2016

Kyle went to our street's block party while I stayed home working on comics.

(it was unseasonably cold, hence the hoodie/blanket combo.)

He came back to use the bathroom and gave me some pilfered snacks.

I brought you something.

I love it when a man pulls cookies from his pocket.

And that's why a 34-year-old ate cookies for dinner in her pj's at 7:30 on a Saturday night.

Just try to step to this.

June 12, 2016
Bowdoin, ME

Going to Reuben & Tessa's farm means playing a lot of games.

Tetris Attack on SNES!

Uno.

Blue

Dammit!

Bananagrams.

June 13, 2016

we had our home inspection today.

Yep, I'm gonna draw so many comics up in here.

June 14, 2016

I spend (arguably) too much time thinking about the house I'm buying.

I wonder what color we'll paint the kitchen.

what if the book case doesn't fit in the library?

BOOP

I can't wait to see the house when it snows!

what if it's HAUNTED?

is that a good or bad thing?

Maybe we should replace the bathroom sink.

what if I don't like living in the house?

seems unlikely, but still.

June 15, 2016

Dracula learned how to eat around the prozac in his wet food.

Check. mate.

So for the last few nights I've been pilling his treats instead.

Advantage: Liz.

But the tables turned once again when I realized he'd been spitting them out on the sly, even though I was holding his mouth shut to make him swallow.

I stepped on a PILL?!

Game over, Prince.

June 16, 2016

At a hotel pool with Joan.
POOL RULES
No RUNNING
NO DIVING
NO CHILDREN UNDER 16 w/o PARENT OR GUARDIAN
ADULTS SHOULD NOT SWIM ALONE
What's up with that sign?

ADULTS SHOULD NOT SWIM ALONE
I agree with it! Why do you think I invited you to come swimming?
Just seems like more of a lifestyle suggestion than a RULE.

Did you notice this sign?
POC
NO RUNN
NO DIVIN
NO CHILD
PARENT O
ADULTS S
ALONE
Catch up, Kyle.

June 17, 2016

I've been burning the candle at both ends for the last few weeks. Working 24 hrs. a week at the library, dealing with all the trips back and forth to Maine involved in buying the house, and spending whatever time is left over catching up on comics.

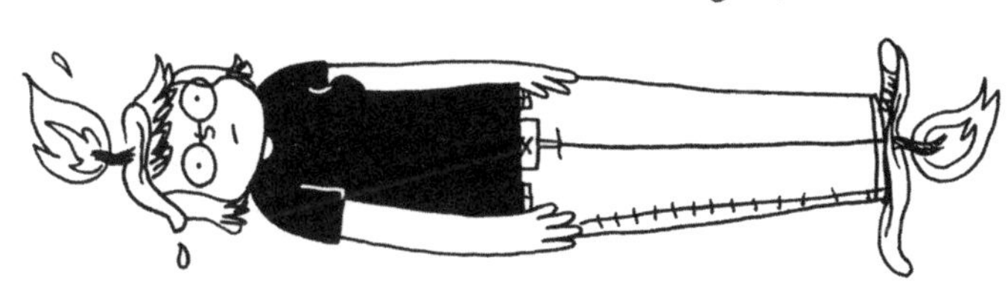

June 18, 2016

I had fun at a cookout with Kyle's family.

You lost! You're my Bocce bitches!

But my mood turned later that night when I was having an "off" drawing day.

Get your act together! I don't have time for this shit!

June 19, 2016
I woke up with a sore throat and was grumpy as fuck about it.
of course NOW I get sick for the first time in 3 years.
It's interesting how quickly I got used to having good days.
FWUMP
WHY ME?!
Bad days feel like an unbearable backslide.
?

June 20, 2016

GROOANN

I still felt pretty cruddy, but I went to my dentist appointment anyway.

June 21, 2016

I see you have an eel tattoo.

I'm a huge fan of anguilliforms. I went on a scuba diving trip and asked the guide if we'd see any murraenidae, which is the Latin name for Moray eels.

June 22, 2016

Are you feeling any better?
Not really.
Try one of my allergy pills, maybe it will help.
it's so tiny.
It worked!
Turns out I wasn't sick, I just have allergies!
...Hey, waitaminute, having allergies is far more annoying...

June 23, 2016

Barker Gee died. He was something of a punk legend in my friend group.

The internet was a pretty sad place today.

But, I mean, if we're being honest, this world is a pretty sad place all the time.

June 24, 2016

A few months ago I got a tiny nip of apple pie-flavored moonshine at the New Hampshire liquor store.

I got it as an impulse buy because the tiny jar was so cute.

Who's a widdle baby booze? It's you! You are!

I decided to bring it to a BBQ that Kyle and I went to.

I only managed to choke down 2 tiny sips before a realization dawned on me.
That was a huge mistake.

June 25, 2016

Woke up hungover from the thimble of moonshine I had last night.

SPEW

Luckily I immediately felt better after honking.

June 26, 2016

More yard sales today. Here's what I got (items not to scale):

An unused still-in-the-box ceiling fan $5

Uno "mod" special edition card game $2

A plastic bag full of real mink scarves $5

"Gatorland" hat $FREE

June 27, 2016

I learned to drive in Santa Fe, where there's never any real traffic, so driving in Boston is something that has always terrified me.

Since I'll likely need a car in Maine, I'm taking steps towards getting comfortable behind the wheel again.

um, maybe I should drive...

you're doing really great.

y'know, I think Zoloft has erased my driving anxiety.

June 28, 2016

I'm just so very tired.

Dear Liz,
concerning your mortgage, we need 12 more documents.
please provide:
1.-paternity test for your great grandfather
a

And it's my least favorite weather: hot & humid.

At least my armpits smell like Indian food.*

*Kyle and I went to Indian buffet early because we're going out of town.

June 29, 2016
Oops! I've been driving in reverse!
MOM!? What's wrong!?
I'm getting arrested because you dented a stranger's car.
Apparently my anxiety about driving has other ways of manifesting.

June 30, 2016

Bye, have fun on tour. I'll miss you!

I'll miss you, too! Love you.

What's the matter? Sad that you're going to be ALONE for 2 weeks?

NO WAY! I'm just overwhelmed by having control over the Netflix.

FWUMP

Ole
Smoky
moonshine

JULY

July 2016

Somerville, MA, U.S.A., Earth

July 11, 2016 Hadley, NY

I hitched a ride to upstate NY with Donna, my older (half) brother's mom.

It started torrentially down-pouring when we got to camp.

Oh well, it's too late to swim anyway.

Then my niece, her friend and I went unsuccessfully toad hunting.

Last year there were a bunch in this leaf litter.

Don't go in there: it's the dogs' bathroom.

Everyone retired to the bunkhouse pretty early.

DONNA

ME

ETHAN & SISTER-IN-LAW LIZ

July 2, 2016
Hadley, NY

July 3, 2016
Hadley, NY

Today a swarm of families from surrounding camps came over for my niece's birthday.

♫ HAPPY BIRTHDAY, DEAR CLEMMA ♫

Too... many... people.

Then we went to a neighboring camp to watch a fireworks display. Every direction you looked there were fireworks across the lake.

July 4, 2016

And spent the rest of the night catching up with my cats.

So, what did you do this weekend?

SNIFF SNIFF

US? You're the one who came home smelling like a campfire!

July 5, 2016
HAPPY BIRTHDAY GRANDMA!
crying
sniffle Thank you, but it's not very happy when you never get to see anyone.
What do you mean? My mom and sister are there almost everyday. Isn't my mom setting up a party for you right now?
Oh, that's right. I always forget. Anyway, how's the baby?
Annnd now she thinks I'm my shitty cousin who has a kid.

July 6, 2016

stupid car that won't stop at the crosswalk. Thanks for NOTHING.

HEEYyyYy GORGEOUS

July 7, 2016

After work I met Jordyn for dinner at Tenóch.

Sorry Kyle, I'm gonna marry this torta.

Then we saw Independence Day: Resurgence.

Some joke that references the first film.

Ha Ha

July 8, 2016

The last time I saw my aunt she randomly said:

All lives matter.

I don't know what prompted it, but I've known for a long time not to engage that part of my family in a political discussion.

...

Her voice is the voice I hear in my head whenever someone argues against the importance of Black Lives Matter.

Trust me, you don't want to agree with my aunt.

ALL LIVES MATTER.

July 9, 2016

I've started doing the Insanity workout again.

I don't really understand why I tend to stop for months at a time, because I always feel much more productive and motivated when I work out on a regular basis.

July 10, 2016

YAY! You're home!

smooch

So, do you want to eat dinner or go right into making out?

Well, this is certainly one of the clearest non-verbal responses I've ever gotten.

July 11, 2016

we stopped trying to give Dracula Prozac a few weeks ago: he was too good at not taking it, and we want to wait and see if having more space in the new house will help the cats be less territorial.

July 12, 2016

My house is cluttered with boxes!

winter clothe

Kitchen

FRAGILE

basement

BOOKS

BOOKS

July 13, 2016

It is currently the morning of July 18th, and I had to put off posting my weekly comic digest because I can't get this day's strip to work.

I wanted to say something poignant about how my good friends just had their second baby, which got me thinking about how the people you love can fall out of your orbit accidentally. It was supposed to be contrasted with running into a close friend whom I'd had a falling out with at the grocery store. For some reason the combinations of the two anecdotes didn't work together, leaving me to conclude that there are just some ideas not suited to this small space.

July 14, 2016
Tonight Kyle and I saw the new Ghostbusters.
CLAP
CLAP
CLAP
CLAP
Oh my god, I LOVED that! Let's see it again right now!
Ha, it was good!
It wasn't a worthy reboot because the SCIENCE wasn't believable.
NY

July 15, 2016

ZZZZZZZZZZZZZZZZZZZZ

July 16, 2016

Porter Sq. vet, what's your emergency.

Um, well, I don't know if it's an emergency, but my cat Dracula might be having a urinary crystal flare up.

Ok, bring him in.

Well, his bladder doesn't feel full, but there's something in there, so I'll be able to take a urine sample.

I'm sorry, Drakey, we just have to make sure there's nothing wrong with your peehole.

Thusly I earned my nickname "Silly Lizzy".

July 18, 2016

This last week sleep has been very difficult.

Oh, good. Another day awake for the sunrise.

Tonight I read about how lunar cycles can disrupt sleep.

Oh wow, it IS almost a full moon!

*not literally literally: internet literally.

July 19, 2016

Hello, Liz? This is Porter Sq. vet. Dracula's urine sample came back clean.

So, then, what was wrong with him?

It's just the mystery of cats.™

I'm really glad you're OK, but I wish you could be mysterious in a less expensive way.

Does this help?

...Yes.

July 20, 2016
I've been pretty obsessed with Wolfman lately.
OMG! You are SO! CUTE!
Like, way more obsessed than usual. Which is saying A LOT.
KISS-KISSY KISS KISS
It's because you hung out with a baby the other day.

July 21, 2016

I'm at the end of my rope as far as my insomnia is concerned.
How am I even still ALIVE?!

July 22, 2016

All of this insomnia and house-buying stuff has prevented me from keeping up on my daily comics.

must... draw... five days... all at... once.

Today I quit my library job two weeks early. I'll have more time to draw, but I'm going to miss being in the stacks.

RIP

WILL SHELVE BOOKS FOR FOOD.

July 23, 2016

We went to pick up some recliners that a friend of Kyle's dad gave to us.

How is it?

ZANG

↑ Genuine LA-Z-BOY

Kyle's dad introduced me as "Kyle's fiance."

...and this is Kyle's fiance, Liz.

Maybe Kyle is **MY** fiance. Ever think of that?

Then we went home and finished Stranger Things.

Ha! That'll be us in the new house.

July 24, 2016

Joel helped me build a lightbox for an arcade marquee that was a birthday gift 5 years ago. Better late than never, but it ended up being one of the hottest days of the year so far. Not ideal weather for woodworking in a backyard for 5 hours.

100°

Hey,

Great work, guys.

BZZZZZZZ

July 25, 2016

I can go a whole day without looking in the mirror.

July 26, 2016

Another day, another pile of boxes appears.

LIZ

LIZ

I'm pretty ready to skip ahead to the actual move.

LIZ

July 27, 2016

I get this feeling of being beaten down by my circumstances, and not being as productive as I'd like in the areas that matter most.

My tendency is to place shame on myself for being un-productive.

I can suffer this way for weeks before I have that "AHA" moment when I realize that I can change my priorities to give more time to the things that matter most to me.

Maybe not immediately, but it gives me something to work towards.

I believe the word used to describe this feeling is "empowered".

It's pretty spot on.

July 28, 2016

The new Descendents record comes out tomorrow.
I thought it comes out on the 29th.

Tomorrow IS the 29th.

MELT

SNAP
SPLAT

July 29, 2016

Kyle & I walked to Shaw's with a bag full of seltzer cans and all the change we've saved for the last few years.
Thanks for carrying everything.
You're welcome.

We used the $2.70 from returning the cans to buy 2 Friendly's sundaes.
Reese's peanut butter cup for Kyle
Friendly's
Ice cream cake for me
Friendly's

We turned the coins into a $73 Home Depot gift card.
EAT MY CANS!
WOW, it says there's 1500 pennies!
CA-CHING
CA-CHING
CA-CHING

July 30, 2016

For the first time in months I'm all caught up on my comics before the weekend! I got to spend the day doing other random chores/projects.

Stained the lightbox Joel and I made last weekend.
I'm probably fucking this up.
Cleaned the recliners we got (they were free for a reason).
Scrub scrub
Ew, the water turned BROWN.
B
Drew a picture of our new house for change of address cards.
Aw, let's put it on the fridge.

July 31, 2016
Wolfman seems to NEED something.
MROW
Hey sweets wanna sit on my lap?
MEOW
Pets?
MROW
Catnip pickle?
MEW
Treats?
MROW
SHAKE SHAKE
LITTLE KITTLES
Naps? You wanna lay down?
MRRW
Laundry pile?
MEOW
DUMP
I'm outta ideas. Money? You want some cash?
MEW

89

AUGUST

SOLD

Home Run
Real Estate

August 2016

Portland, ME, U.S.A., Earth

August 1, 2016

I worked really fast to get my July patreon books laid out and printed before my hectic upcoming weekend.

Kyle & I ate dinner at the Border Cafe while my books printed.

The food here is super whatever.

Yeah.

But the margaritas are great!

Yeah!

clink

And might've maybe gotten a little drunk accidentally.

At home I made a troubling discovery.

Why are there comics from MAY in this book!?

This really harshes my buzz.

August 2, 2016

Here's a breakdown of what happened with July misprint:

I used the layout of May's book as a template for July, because they have the same number of days.

MAY
31

I print my books doubled on the page, front & back, so they can be easily collated by the photo-copier. when I use an older issue as a template I paste the new comics over the old, using the previous dates as a guide.

JULY
31

I forgot to paste July's comics over the bottom half of the May 9th & May 22nd page, so now I have to reprint that page.

D'oh!

August 3, 2016

Today Joel and I did another woodworking project.

well, this is both terrifying and awesome.

Baby's first time using a rotary saw.

BZZZZZT

We made a coffin-shaped cat bed!

It's kinda hard to believe it worked!

I wonder if any neighbors caught a glimpse of our handiwork.

What the fuck?...

August 4, 2016
Z

August 5, 2016

Friends came over to help us paint our new house today.

Danny

Megan

AUGUST 6TH 2016

Guest comic by Danny Bailey! Thanks Danny!

LIZ IS TOO BUSY BEING A HOMEOWNER TO MAKE A COMIC TODAY SO HERES MINE!

I WORKED!

I HELPED LIZ AND MEGAN PAINT!

I PICNIC'D

OOOH ART!

I BAILED ON FUNTOWN!

SAD MEGAN PANTS

THEN LIZ + KYLE TALKED ME INTO DRIVING SOME NASTY TRASH TO MY APARTMENT DUMPSTER!

August 7, 2016

I have 3 blisters on my right hand from gripping a paint roller all damn weekend.

I drove back to Boston: still gaining confidence behind the wheel.

YAY LIZ!

I just used a TOLL BOOTH!

Good for you.

B

It's our last trash night in Somerville, so we put my armchair out on the curb. RIP armchair.

why are you crying?

The cats LOVE that chair!

August 8, 2016

In life there will always be plans that, despite our best intentions, never come to fruition. One perk of moving is that it's motivation to actually act on some of those back-burner hangouts.

Brutal.

I rolled another 1, so I'm gonna fireball...

Dammit, not me again.

Is this one of those passive-agressive relationship things?

August 9, 2016

She's moving. She should be HAPPY.

More like disgusted by the mortgage industry.

I think she should be scared: what if her house is haunted?!

SKA!

BANE

She should be ANGRY that Somerville is so unaffordable to people like her!

Or sad that she's leaving a place with so many memories.

SKA!

Goddamn. What a HEADACHE.

I think it was a floor model? It has a price tag.
It was in the 50% off section.

Too punx 4 Ikea.

August 11, 2016

Today was my last therapy session for awhile.

I don't want to make a big show of this, but I do want to say that it's been an honor to work with you. Your dedication to self-improvement and self-reflection is inspiring.

You are a very thoughtful person.

I don't think I've ever had my inner life so understood and validated.

Oh, wow, thank you. That means a lot.

Oddly, I wasn't moved to tears until I was leaving the building.

Someone knows how much work I do.

August 12, 2016

Before I moved from Santa Fe to Boston in 2002 I felt a profound sense of loss.

I don't want to leave this city: a city where I know all the best shortcuts like my own secrets*

GARFIELD

Why am I even going to Boston? I love my comm-unity here! I'll miss my friends!

PS

Hey! There you are! Get in!

How did you know where I was!?

Well, I know your shift at Video Library ended at 3, and I saw your car at Warehouse, so I knew you'd be walking back there, and I know you like to take side streets...

I'll miss THIS.

* I was 20 years old and really emo. Gimme a break.

August 13, 2016

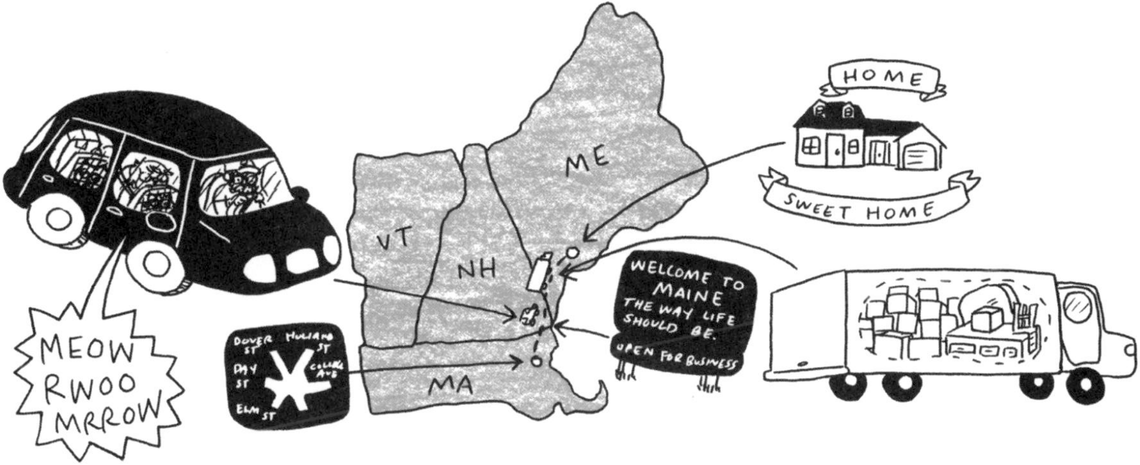

MEOW RWOO MRROW

DOVER ST
HOLLAND ST
DAY ST
COLLEGE AVE
ELM ST

VT
NH
ME
MA

WELCOME TO MAINE
THE WAY LIFE SHOULD BE.
OPEN FOR BUSINESS

HOME
SWEET HOME

Happy Birthday Claire!

August 14, 2016

August 15, 2016
Before I moved, my therapist and I talked about routine, as I'm someone who needs routine.
BARF. who lets their kitchen get this dirty?
It's a double-edged sword: my problem is more that I fall into routine too readily.
All right! which room am I cleaning today?!
BEEP BEEP BEEP
SPROING
8:00
I've been packing and cleaning and unpacking and cleaning for so long that it's become my new normal, making some more important things alien.
um, hello?
You're supposed to DRAW on me!

August 16, 2016

Once I stayed at an Air BNB and the host told me that if I was going to cook, not to buy any spices, because he has "every spice." When I opened his cupboard, there were only, like, 10 spices in there.

...10 is not a lot of spices.

Where are we going to put all these?!

August 17, 2016

Although our house is still mostly in boxes, we had Megan, Danny, and Matt over for dinner.

veggie burgers with lettuce, tomato, pickles, cheese, and shaved red onion

"Princeton whole earth salad" with kale, cabbage, brown rice, dill, parsley, and a garlic, tamari, mustard dressing.'

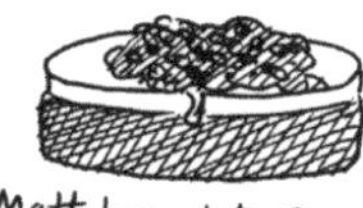
Matt brought a Daiya cheesecake.

Megan made vegan, gluten free peanut butter brownies.

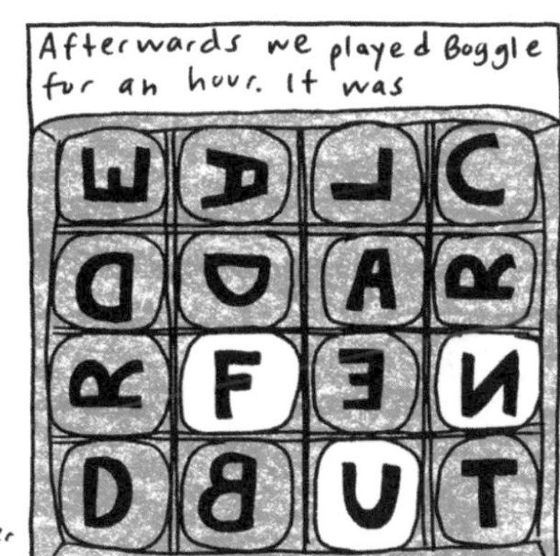

August 18, 2016

we got dinner with some friends from Philly who live in Portland.

Karen

Peter

The only person who got dessert

And took an after-dinner stroll that ended up at Arcadia.

GHOST BUSTERS

U SUCK

WOW. I'm so bad at this!

August 19, 2016
I'm very frustrated by my house's state of disarray.
LIZ OFFICE
PAPER
LIZ TOYS 1
LIZ TOYS 2
LIZ OFFICE
STAPLER
light box
desk lamp
STOP STARING AT ME!!

Kyle and Liz ride the Excalibur at Funtown in pitch blackness.

August 20 2016

AHHHHHHHHH

CLACK CLACK CLACKCLACK

IT'S SO DARK!

CLACK CLACK CLACKCLACK

WHY WON'T IT END ALREADY?!

CLACK CLACK CLACKCLACK

CLACKCLACK HALT

OH GOD! MY NECK!

August 21, 2016
I got inspired to paint the kitchen today.
Sometimes I just need the satisfaction of completeing a tedious task,
Just one more coat on the trim, then I can roll!
Just to see the end result.
No! Wolfman!

August 22, 2016

I've been forgetting to take my anxiety meds.

PUSH & TURN
OPEN
CLOSE
PRINCE
SERTALINE
100 MG TABLET

Why is "unlikable" my brain's default?

August 23, 2016

I took an 8am train to Boston and got to sit in an observation car that's temporarily on the Downeaster line.

After a long day in Boston, I met up with Kyle and drove us home taking Storrow Drive for the first time while he ate tacos in the passenger seat.

EXP'WAYS 1 28 NORTH

DOWNTOWN BOSTON

This is pure terror.

sorry

August 24, 2016

Wolfman has a new late night game: she runs down the stairs making a guttural scream, turning the stairwell into an echo chamber.

GROOWWOOOROOOAAAROWLLL

Then she dives into the rocking recliner full force, causing it to slam into the base repeatedly.

BOUNCE

CLANG

CLANG

While she races back upstairs to do it all over again.

GROWAAAOWW

Is this real?

'Fraid so.

CLANG

CLANG

August 25, 2010
Green Bay, WI

I flew from Portland to Green Bay. At my hotel:

...Hello?

Hi Liz, this is the front desk. I forgot to tell you that you've been selected as our "guest of the day"!

The "guest of the day" gets a free beverage and snack from the lobby market.

Are you sure that's what you want? You can get Hot Pockets or an ice cream...

This is good.

Thanks.

Lemon water

Heath bar

HEATH

Alec, Claire, Suzanne, and Nicole all got in at around midnight.

Suzanne cried for 1/2 of our flight.

I read about that on twitter!

August 26, 2016
Green Bay, WI

I felt really dysmorphic in the dress I packed for Aaron & Jessica's wedding reception.

I was looking forward to escaping into alcohol, but at the venue I discovered that they only had beer & wine*. A good samaritan friend of Aaron's stepdad drove me to a grocery store.

Is this the smallest whiskey you sell?

yes.

Someone likes to party!
...or I'm running from negative thoughts, duder.

Are you feeling any better?
Well, everyone thinks I have an alcohol problem, but yes.

* both make me sick :(

Green Bay, WI

There was a picnic lunch on a boat as the final event of the wedding reception.

RIVER TYME

My flight home was an hour late, so I didn't get in until 1am. Kyle accidentally fell asleep and didn't pick me up until 2.

I can't tell if being the only person here makes this better, or worse.

August 28, 2016

The bleacher seats at today's Seadogs game really hurt my ass.

I don't even like watching baseball.

Afterwards we took one of our patented naps.

MPH. Nap first, sexy time afterwards.

Then I inked a whole week's worth of comics while watching old Masterchef episodes.

How Liz Prince got her groove back.

FINALLY.

August 29, 2016

Danny and I went on a Mondate to the thrift store.

Should I get this shirt?

It's a very Liz shirt!

August 30, 2016

When I was in Green Bay, Kyle found a tree frog on our rain barrel.

August 31, 2016
Today we hit the farmer's market.
Can we get this watermelon? It has an umbilical cord.
B

We took a walk on the Eastern Promenade.
Wow, that's an atomic blast of bird shit.

For some reason we got take out for dinner even though we have a lot of stuff to cook with.

SEPTEMBER

September 2016

Portland, ME, U.S.A., Earth

September 1, 2016

my nap game is on point.

I don't want to sleep through this!

... well not so much for actual napping...

September 2, 2016

Kyle's going to Boston tonight, maybe we should go with him!

No. We don't need to go to Boston. We need to draw our comics.

Aw, c'mon! We can eat at Shake Shack!

NO.

SHAKE SHACK!

Later...

Thank god we didn't go to Boston. This is MUCH better.

SHut up and eat your leftovers. I can't hear masterchef.

September 3, 2016

September 4, 2016

Today Kyle's mom & stepdad came over for a cookout on our opulent back deck.

But we don't have any deck furniture yet.

September 5, 2016

If you're in the market for a vacuum, do yourself a favor and get one from Best Buy with a 2-year protection plan.

And this piece fell off.*
Our vacuum stopped working.*
Ok, here's a credit for $106 towards a new vacuum.**
Thanks!
BEST BUY
Welp, another year, another free vacuum.***
And we still have $10 on this card!
BEST BUY
HOOVER PET
WIND TUNNEL

* Both true! We're not scammers

** You can spend it on ANYTHING.

*** Technology doesn't last longer than 2 years.

September 6, 2016

Today I'm a walking contradiction.

GRIND

GRIND

GRIND

There's a lot of things I want to do, but don't feel motivation to do, and there's no time to wallow in feeling unmotivated.

GRIND

CLENCH

GRIND

OK, so I'm really more of a laying-around-complaining contradiction.

GROSS THINGS I DID TODAY (an exposé)

September 7, 2016

1. Picked wolfman's nose

SQUIRM

2. Looked at the booger under a microscope.

Holy crap! That's awful!

3. Bought Maple Bacon flavor Pop-tarts.

4. Ate maple bacon flavor Pop-tarts.

Holy crap! That's awful!

September 8, 2016

I went to a last-minute Hannibal Buress show @ Port City Music Hall with Reuben & Tessa.

I'm sorry, I can't do any of those. Right now I'm doing 'stand up for my mortgage.'

I have a mortgage! I get that joke!

HA HA HA HA HA HA

September 9, 2016

Danny showed me a swimming spot close to my house.

wouldn't it be great if there were kittens on inner tubes in this river?

you should make your comic about that!

Megan came over and we got Lib's.

They put candy eyes on our cones!

Then we got Little Caesar's and watched SLC Punk 2.

This movie really, really sucks.

mhm

September 10, 2016

Then we went to Bullmouse and I bought maybe too many books.

September 11, 2016
Mike & Jeanne stayed over at our house last night. Today we dicked around downtown.
BOOTH SERVICE
Portland
BOOTH SERVICE
B
MONSTER EMPORIUM
COAST CITY COMICS
THE GREEN HAND
METAL

September 12, 2016

I've been solidifying this idea the last year that it's ok to let people have their emotional reactions without trying to change their minds.

A good example is when Kyle fell asleep when he was supposed to pick me up.*

It was an accident, don't be mad!

You're allowed to make a mistake, but I'm allowed to be upset about it.

I exercised my right to anger again tonight.

Sorry, I just don't want to pain tonight. I worked all day–

You're allowed to not participate: I started this project myself but I'm still going to be disap–pointed.

*see August 27th's comic.

September 13, 2016

Mike & Jeanne are in town again: today we went to Mackworth Island.

wow, this snake skin is really fresh!

I hope we don't run into its previous owner!

We saw some really impressive fairy houses there.

This one has a pool! I bet the fairies fight over who gets to live in it.

METAL

It was nice to finally spend a day outdoors, I mean, I live in Maine for christsakes.

September 14, 2016

The doctor's think my grand-mother's dementia is actually Alzheimer's.

They think she's had it for 8 or 9 years!

Fuck, mom, that's really serious!

Alzheimer's is the disease I'm most afraid of: you lose your memory and your motor functions. Basically, your brain shuts your body down by forgetting how to run it.

I was really hoping we wouldn't have Alzheimer's in our bloodline.

I've done a fair amount of reading on the subject, but I don't remember if there's a heredity connection.

My self care in this situation is to NOT look that up.

September 15, 2016

Our mortgage company invited its clients on a sunset cruise around Casco Bay.

There was an open bar.

Hi, I'd like a cider.

Can I get a whisky and coke?

TIPS

And surprisingly classy food.

veggie sushi

pasta salad

kale orzo salad

We ate a lot and drank a lot and didn't talk to anyone.

A perfect night.

September 16, 2016

I often think about how famous I want to be by measuring myself against other cartoonists.

It's an aspirational thing, not a jealousy thing*.

* sometimes a jealousy thing.

Raina Telgemeier is the highest echelon of graphic novelist fame, but since her fans are middle-grade readers, their interactions are kinda needy.

LOLgrrl2005
First like!

dR@mAQWN
Raina! I love your books. Please follow me,back it would mean everything! This is the 3rd time I've asked :(

kitty133491827448

I only get a small fraction of that from my Tomboy readers, but it's already so hard to set boundaries with fans who are so young.

Dear Liz, OMG! I can't Believe you replied to my email! Please write back to this one too, I need to hear from you!

your fan,
Josie

September 17, 2016

Got chairs for the backyard

Red plastic

Then got home to realize that I needed a special Screwdriver called a Robertson head, so I went right back to the hardware store.

Homeowner life.

September 18, 2016

The previous owners of our house had a very different sense of design than Kyle and I do, so there were a lot of rooms that needed to be painted over, but none as desperately as our basement, which we dubbed the "Serengeti Sunset."

Before.

During.

After.

September 19, 2016

I've been working really hard to set up the house because my mom is visiting next week. Today I focused on my office.

Part of the process involves cataloging my old artwork.
Reading through a lot of my comics, enough time has elapsed that I don't hate them anymore.
So that's nice.

September 20, 2016

September 21, 2016

In addition to falling leaves, our yard is currently besieged by falling acorns.

PING!

OW!

Having an acorn pelt your head is admittedly pretty funny, but it also really hurts.

Ethan came up from Providence for the night, and after an awesome dinner out, we had drinks on my newly pinterest-ified back deck.

I feel like I should be concerned about acorns.

That's real!

September 22, 2016

Danny and I went on a mega Halloween shopping spree.

Spirit had the best socks (maybe ever).

BRAINS!

EYES!

Goodwill had lots of cool old lights and assorted decor.

This will be a year-round accent piece in my home.

HOW-TO

BEASTS

SPELLS

Christmas Tree shop had plastic skeleton arm salad servers that I'm going to stick in my yard.

Earlier in the day the Google street view car drove down our street.

NO! NOT YET! my decorations aren't up!

Google maps street view

The thought pattern brought me to realize 2 times about myself:

1: I've become very accustomed to living in the present.

And 2: I'm really freaked about how our minds can manipulate our reality.

September 24, 2016

We go to Home Depot at least once a week now.

Maybe we should just move in here, we visit so damn much.

THE HOME DEPOT

I mean I don't mind it, if we're being honest.

OH MY GOD! That's brilliant! We're getting one!

LEAF CHU

Lawn & Refuse bag

But when does the hemorrhaging money part of owning a home stop?

HACK You're killin' me! cough

PAFF

we silently declared today the last of the big shopping ventures. Now our finished basement is outfitted to be a guest room for when my mom visits.
September 25, 2016
throw blanket
Floor lamp
STREET TRASH
New TV
Area rug
TV stand

September 26, 2016

It got very fall-esque overnight.

MMM, Fall clothes.

Sit down, please!

Wolfman is now magnettic-ally attracted to me.

MMM, cat cuddles.

You'd better not even think about getting up.

And for the first time in my adult life I live somewhere with a working fireplace.

MMM, living my best life.

OUR best life.

September 27, 2016

Today was a pretty stark contrast to how cozy I felt yesterday.

Knead Knead

PURRRRRRRRRRRRRRR

I feel conflicted about how much you enjoy my debilitating cramps.

September 28, 2016

I acted like a ding dong at the DMV.

I can't see the light! I have no peripheral vision?!

I keep telling you! you're looking in the WRONG place!

After frantically cleaning the house, I met Megan & Danny at Friendly's...

From now on I'm only eating food shaped like a vampire.

which is conveniently airport-adjacent, because I had a special delvery to pick up.

MOMMY!

LIZZY!

September 29, 2016

I was excited to show my mom around the city I now call home,

It's a store that just sells novelty socks!

That's perfect for you!

THE SOC SHACK

WE'RE OPEN

but probably more excited to have her at my house.

CRACKLE

POP

CRACKLE

September 30, 2016

Kyle and I got married at city hall with our moms as our witnesses.

And do you, Kyle, take Liz to be your spouse?

I DO.

Liz and Kyle

Then we went on a lobster boat tour.

These two got married today, so they're gonna help me show you how to sex a lobster.

OCTOBER

October 2016

Portland, ME, U.S.A., Earth

October 1, 2016

When it's rainy and gloomy out, you're gonna need to get some supplies...

onions

fresh dill

weird/pretty mushrooms

Hungarian paprika

veggie boullion

butter

sour cream

SOUR CREAM

tiny milk

VITAMIN WHAT EVER

S

P

salt & pepper

...to make soup!

October 2, 2016
At breakfast in Belfast, ME
...and here is your breakfast burrito.
This is the breakfast burrito? These are TACOS!
Welcome to Maine: the whitest state in America!
HA HA HA*
* laughing on the outside, crying on the inside

October 3, 2016

Danny and I packaged the enamel pins we designed together for her brand pindigogrrrls.

Haha! These are so cute!

KA-CHUNK

They **ARE** cute.

FUCKEN' BERRY
FUCKY U BERRY MUCH

check out pindigogrrrls.storenvy.com

But I get really stressed about commerce, especially when someone else is backing it.

KA-CHUNK

But what if no one else thinks they're cute?

October 4, 2016

People keep congratulating me on getting married.

CONGRATULATIONS!

heh, thanks.

I love my ~~boyfriend~~ husband, but marriage has never felt romantic to me.

Isn't it perhaps MORE romantic to stay together without a legal obligation?

*

* Yes, we are wearing rings to see if we like it/if it feels symbolic to us.

I should probably translate a wedding congrats into a congrats for cultivating a nurturing chosen family,

because that really is something worth celebrating.

October 5, 2016

An outdoor cat got too close to the house and it caused Wolfman & Dracula to fight.

HISS

YOWL CLAW SPIT

It's called "redirected aggression" and it's not the first time that it's happened with my cats.

Do you think it's time to revisit the idea of finding Dracula a one-cat household to live in? Wolfman is so aggressive towards him, he'd probably do better without her around.

I know that it's selfish of me to keep him here, but I don't want him to live somewhere else! But you're right that he'd be happier without Wolfman constantly bullying him. I don't know what to do, though.

October 6, 2016

The cats are being separated; Wolfman in the basement, Dracula in the main house.

October 7, 2016

October 8, 2016
Danny and I went to a FREE showing of BeetleJuice at the Saco Drive-in!
TACO BELL
ok, so this is the worst foreshortening ever.

October 9, 2016

Today I drove a road I'd only ever been on with you,
Red's Eats

to go to a place I'd probably never heard of if I hadn't visited it with you all those years we were close friends.

S. FERNALD'S

I thought it'd be painful to occupy a space I'd only ever existed in with you, but I'm past the place where your memory hurts.

I'm in a place where I can look back and smile.

October 10, 2016

If I wake up in the middle of the night, I can easily fall back asleep.

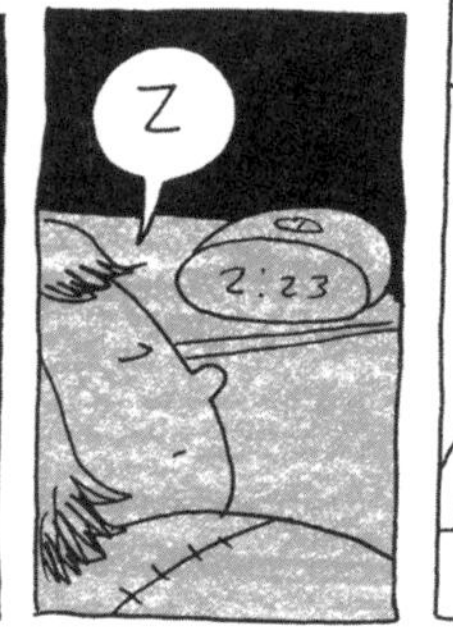

October 11, 2016

There is some lingering aggression from the cat fight last week.

Seriously?! He's just sitting there doing **NOTHING**.

HISSSSSSSSSSSSSSSS

I was feeling grumpy and unproductive, so we went out for thai food.

DROWN YOUR TROUBLES

IN A

BIG BOWL OF TOM YUM SOUP.

Then I bought the new Ghostbusters on Blu-Ray.

This is the first time I've bought a new movie in years!

GHOSTBUSTERS

October 12, 2016

Rode the bus to Boston and met Jordyn for dinner.

I wonder if us wearing wedding rings and having dinner together makes people assume we're married to EACH OTHER.

Wow, we'd be some serious doppelbangers!

I spilt water on my lap as we were paying the check.

AW, dang it!

CLUNK

Just in time for me to go interview Box Brown at Brookline Booksmith in front of an audience.

Tetris Tetris Tetris

Having a wet crotch at public events is becoming my brand!*

TETRIS

TOMBOY

* see January 21st's comic

October 13, 2016

You haven't really lived

until you've walked the perimeter of your yard,

Sprinkling it with urine-soaked cat litter to ward off outdoor cats.

Maybe my vet is playing a practical joke on me.

October 14, 2016

sorry Patrons! :(

October 15, 2016

PRESENTING MY TECHNIQUE FOR ROASTING MARSHMALLOWS:

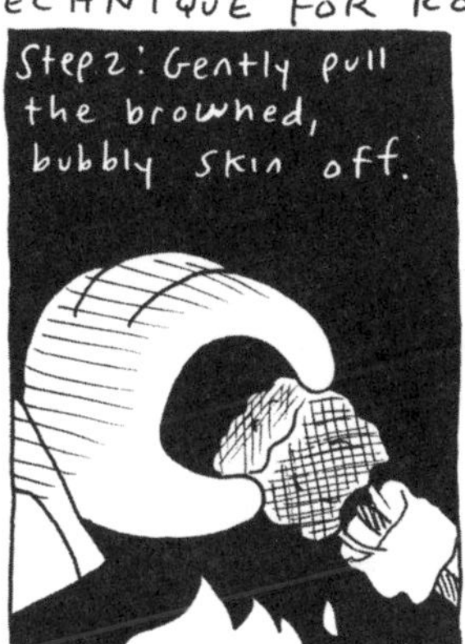

October 16, 2016

The Simpsons Treehouse of Horror is historically my favorite TV event of the year.

HOW TO COOK FOR FORTY HUMANS

But the last few years?

A James Bond parody?

I think they're mis-taking GORE for HORROR.

October 17, 2016

I've been pretty down on myself lately because aside from these daily comics, I'm not producing anything at the moment. I feel like I'm being lazy, except that when I'm not drawing, I'm working on setting up and cleaning the house, responding to emails, and running errands. If we're being honest, I haven't even had time to be lazy! So why am I such a jerk to myself?!

October 18, 2016

Based on yesterday's revelation, I decided to take a hot bath to relax. I even got a bath bomb for the first time.

Turns the water fizzy? I wanna take a seltzer bath!

But by the time the tub was 1/4 full the water had stopped coming out of the faucet hot.

Well, there goes that idea. I'm not relaxing in a tepid pool of my own filth.

unused

I was greeted at the bathroom door by a huge wet cat puke.

Oh. Good.

I missed you. ♡

At least I didn't step in it, I guess.

October 19, 2016

Kyle's dad came up with some tools and we spent the day doing projects.

I pressure washed the deck.

Gas fumes

This thing makes me feel like a Ghostbuster!

WHIRR

BLAST

While Kyle and his dad removed some molding and drywall from above the refrigerator,

I think there's ANOTHER nail in there.

SHIT!

And cut a hole in the basement wall, leading to an unused closet that I'm going to turn into a cat bathroom.

This is where you'll poop now.

?

October 20, 2016
I helped Danny paint her new bedroom.
Totally
The guy at Lowe's said this color is "Simpsons radioactive green".
And moved some of her stuff in, and built cube shelves, too
Thank god these are light or we'd have to call a MAN.
HA HA HA
And then I went home and helped Kyle bag leaves.
#1 HELPER
Snow shovel

October 21, 2016
I think your Halloween decorations might've scared a little kid last night.
Oh?
(next door neighbor)
There was a couple pushing a stroller down the street...
and when they got to your house the kid started SCREAMING!
WAHHHHHH
I thought my yard was pretty benign, but I can't say I'm not proud.

October 22, 2016

Our friend Matt organizes big horror movie screenings, usually as camp-outs, but because of the torrential rain, tonight's is in an awesome wood-paneled basement.

October 23, 2016

The cats had another big fight today, this time over "territory" (aka the bed).

STOP IT!

STOP!

FUCK, YOU!

NO, FUCK YOU!

Dracula was sequestered in the basement for the rest of the day, but I let him out after about 6 hours.

MMMRRRRRRROOOOWWWW

Kyle and I are rewatching The Wire.

They're out there warrin' over corners!

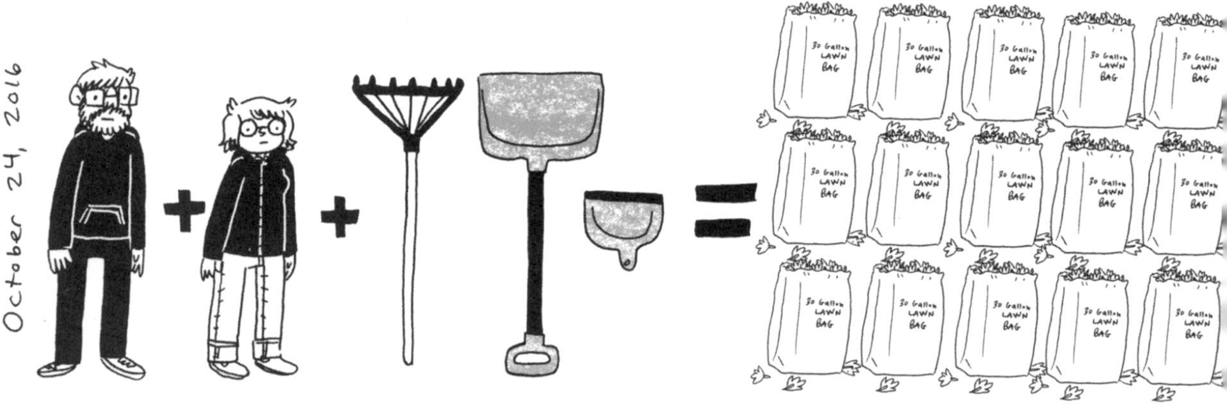

October 24, 2016

30 Gallon LAWN BAG

October 25, 2016

I brought the recycling back in from the curb.

Aaanndd that's the only time I went outside.

October 26, 2016

October 27, 2016

spent a lot of time today trying to get the cats to utilize the cat tree.

You can sit up high and your sister can't get you!

That night I went out for ramen, played pinball, and saw the remastered version of Phantasm.

I'm not into that movie, sorry every horror fan ever.

October 28, 2016

We drove to Ipswich to pick up Kyle's parents' cat, then drove her to Amherst to stay with Kyle's sister. It took 4 hours.

NY
VT
NH
ME
PORTLAND
MA
IPSWICH
AMHERST
CT
RI

I foolishly got a salted caramel cappucino at a gas station. It was a terrible life choice.

This is making me car sick.

Sounds great.

HELP! I'm BEING CAT-NAPPED!

October 29, 2016

Kyle's sister and her wife are having a baby.

Do you hope you get a niece or a nephew, get uncle Kyle?

A niece for sure.

They had a party to reveal whether it would be a boy or a girl.

who wants to know?

Red Velvet = Boy

CARROT = GIRL

October 30, 2016
I don't think it's a good idea for them to sit at the screen door together.
Aw, but they love watching the leaves.
20 minutes later.
STOP! You're proving Kyle RIGHT!
YOWL
SNARL
And so the separation routine begins again.
What am I gonna do, Dracula? This has to stop.
happy because we're alone
PURRRRRRRRRRRRR

October 31, 2016
TRICK OR TREAT!
Here you go. Enjoy!
Thank you.
?

DON'T WORRY! THEY'RE FAKE!

PIRATES OF THE CARIBBEAN
TWILIGHT ZONE
CURIO SHOP
MAINE SQUEEZES
MAINE SQUEEZES

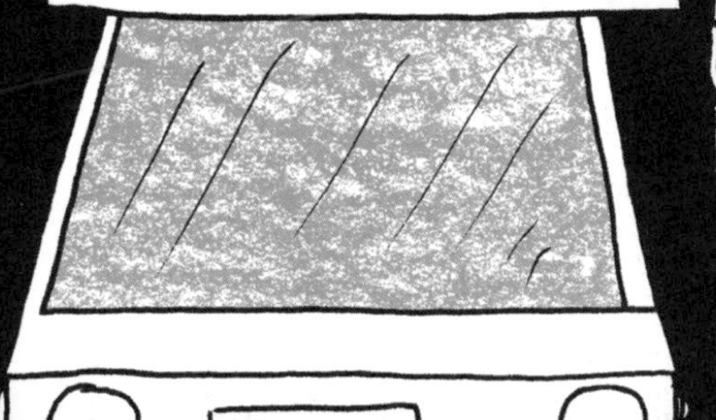

NOVEMBER

November 2016

Portland, ME, U.S.A., Earth

November 1, 2016

Cruddy day wherein I felt cruddy. I seem to have a low-level cold that's lasted for a few weeks.

HONK

The cats are still being aggressive towards each other.

I'm right here, y'know.

HISSSSSSSSS

HISSSSSSSSSSSS

Ended up watching game 5 of the world series.

November 2, 2016

I met up with Megan at Arcadia to practice my pinball skills. We're joining a women's pinball league.

November 3, 2016

How to make vegetarian fajitas

Thinly slice 3 bell peppers (of any color: mix & match!) and 1 red onion. Set aside in a large bowl.

In a mixing bowl whisk together:

2 minced garlic cloves
2 tablespoons fresh cilantro
1/3 cup of fresh lime juice
2 teaspoons cumin
1 teaspoon each of S&P
1/4 cup of water
1 teaspoon oregano

Pour marinade over the sliced peppers and onions, cover, and let sit in the fridge for 6 hours.

Stir fry the veggies with the fake meat of your choice!

Serve on warm flour tortillas with cheese, sour cream, and salsa.

ENJOY!

November 4, 2016

dear Twitter, one would think that with all your algorithms to determine what I want to see,

What's wrong?

I'm just upset with myself.

You'd be able to figure out that if I used to follow somebody and then stopped,

I saw something online that had nothing to do with me, but it made my old intrusive thoughts return.

I don't want their tweets to show up in my feed as a tweet that people I follow have liked.

I felt like I was doing so well and now I'm not.

November 5, 2016

Sometimes you just gotta saw the legs of a thrifted couch with Megan Pants.

This rules!

Can I try?

VRRT

Awesome!

VRRRRRT

It's really fun! Do you want to try?

NOPE.

November 6, 2016

Got brunch with our friends Erin & Dave who are in town.

Oh holy hell, I love eating

Jalapeno bloody mary

cheesy broccoli potato scramble

we also went on a hike, but it was windy and drizzling.

I just can't stop thinking about that breakfast.

November 7, 2016

I tried to watch a documentary about cats called "The Lion In Your Living Room".

Cats are solitary creatures.

Cute, Dracula.

... for everyone involved.

OK! I GET IT!

HISSSSSS

SWAT

November 8, 2016

I was in the basement putting together my October books and watching Simpsons DVDs. At around 10:30 I went upstairs to check on the incoming election results.

270 270

207 244

CLINTON TRUMP

Wait... is DONALD TRUMP going to be PRESIDENT?!

...somehow, yes.

I shoulda just stayed downstairs.

November 9, 2016

My social media feed was very somber today: we're all shocked at the outcome of the election. But it's a poignant reminder that our social circles do not necessarily represent a full range of political leanings.

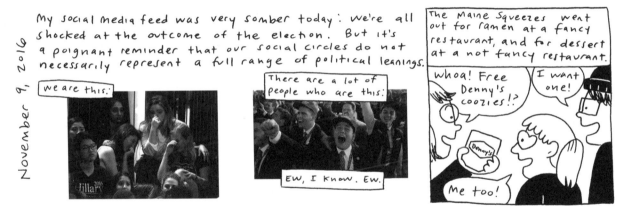

we are this:

Hillary 2016

There are a lot of people who are this:
EW, I know. EW.

The Maine Squeezes went out for ramen at a fancy restaurant, and for dessert at a not fancy restaurant.

Whoa! Free Denny's coozies!?

I want one!

Denny's

Me too!

November 10, 2016

I have been on a regimen where I <u>NEED</u> to take a nap everyday, sometimes for over an hour. My nightly sleep schedule is the best it's ever been, I'm just very low energy throughout the day. I'm a little worried that this is a new side effect of the Zoloft I've been taking for a year, but whatever it is, I feel a lot of shame whenever I succumb to the need to sleep, because upstairs Kyle is working remotely for his QA job.

But the sun sets at, like, 4:30 now, so nature stuff is out of the question.

So we do the opposite of a nature thing...

Ugh, all of these curtains are expensive and ugly.

So, to Bed, Bath, and Beyond?

Thus, with minimal outside help, we changed the tire ourselves.

November 13, 2016

My grandma fell and broke her hip; she needs minor surgery to fix it.

I feel badly for Grandma, but mostly I'm sorry that you can't catch a break on this, mom.

Kyle's friend invited us to his house out in the country, but failed to mention that his driveway is a mile-long treacharous dirt road.

narrow road

hill

ford fiesta

small cliff

big rocks

deep ruts

Tonight was the first meet-up of Belles and Chimes ANB, my local chapter of a national women's pinball league.

I'm excited to learn new tricks from other ladies!

November 14, 2016

When I was a toddler, I had my own nickname for the full moon.

HAMBURGER MOON!

November 15, 2016

November 16, 2016

Reuben, Tessa, and I went on an impromptu dinner date at Empire, an upscale Chinese restaurant that has become my favorite place to eat in Portland.

This is crazy good.

The cats are starting to get the hang of the cat tree.

November 17, 2016
cute.
cute.
Not cute.
HISSSSSSSSSSS

November 18, 2016

November 19, 2016

I'm creating characters and a world for someone else to draw, and I'm having a lot of fun with it!

November 20, 2016

November 21, 2016

Megan was having a bad day.

Danny and I decided to overwhelm her with pies, which we left on her doorstep.

Megan, This is a gift,
Don't be alarmed.
BANANAS

Our stealthy pie mission worked, and as an added bonus, Megan brought the pies over to my house, for a pajama pie party.

← Apple
← Cherry
← Blueberry
← stylish kigurumi

November 22, 2016

November 23, 2016

Browsing the teen graphic novel section at the Portland Public library.

Hey Liz

The librarian just randomly came up to me and said "If you're looking for Tomboy, it's in the adult section!"

It's true! I saw it!

...Did you just get... gender profiled?

November 24, 2016

November 25, 2016

There was a miscommunication and I thought my brother's family was coming up today.
It's almost 1 and they said they'd be here at 11. Should I be worried?

No big deal, most days are interchangable to me.
Now I have time for my daily nap.

But is that sad or awesome?
Drawing in my PJs at 7pm.
I guess my outlook really depends on the day.

November 26, 2016

Ethan, Liz, and Clemma visited today (not yesterday, but you already knew that).

We went to the crypto-zoology museum.

Looked in some bookstores.

I'm looking for a small dictionary so when I'm reading and I find a word I don't know, I can look it up.

My niece is as tall as me!

Then watched the new Ghostbusters at my house.

It's so cute when she walks down the stairs!

Yeeahhh

November 27, 2016

The third week of pinball league was tonight. I've done progressively worse each week.

[illegible]	14	14	16	
[illegible]	6	6	8	
[illegible]	10	14	14	
[illegible]	9	14	9	
[illegible]				
[illegible]	7	8	6	
Liz Prince	12	9	9	
[illegible]		7	12	
[illegible]		7	12	
[illegible]	6	11	10	
[illegible]		17	18	
[illegible]	5		10	
[illegible]	14	11		

But when I play on my own I'm much better than I used to be.

Holy shit! I completed the seance!
KNOCK KNOCK KNOCK

November 28, 2016

Today is Megan's birthday!

Open it!

I don't want to!

HAPPY BIRTHDAY

Do it!

I ruined it by beating her at bowling. *

But it's my birthday!

YEAH!

* by, like, 7 points.

November 29, 2016

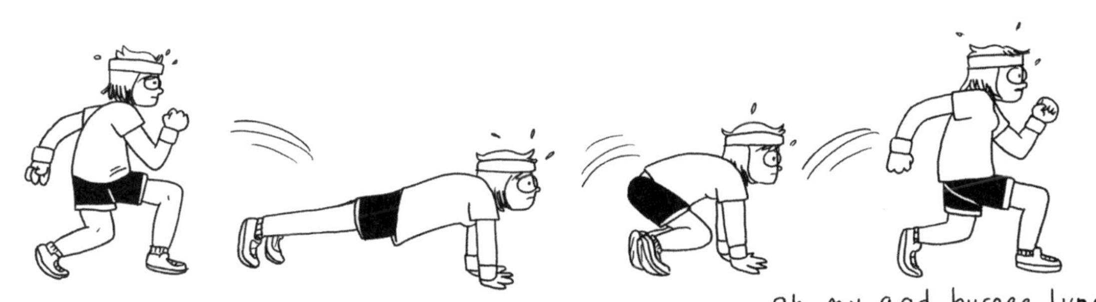
...oh my god, burpee lunges.

November 30, 2016

It's been hard to get myself out of bed. I'm not depressed exactly, I just crave the extra comfort, lately.

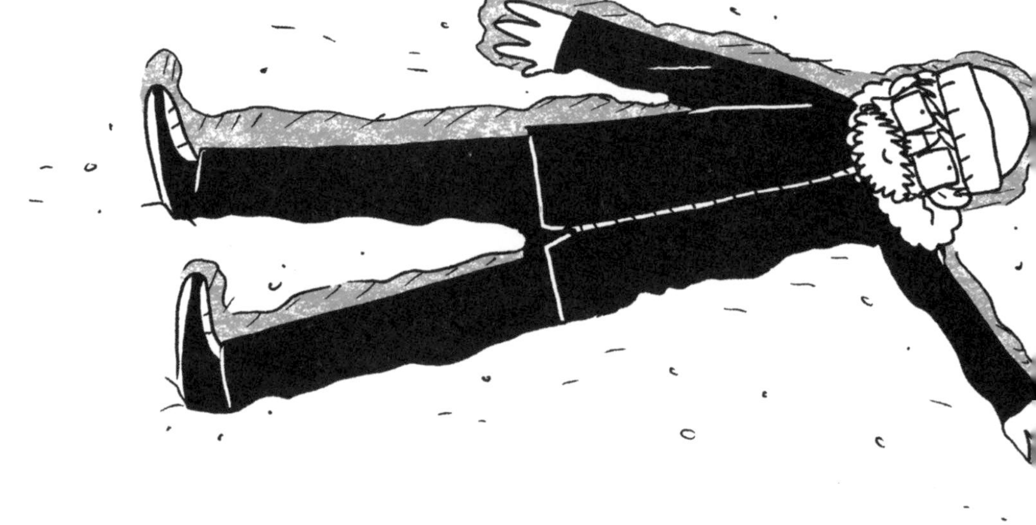

DECEMBER

December 2016

Portland, ME, U.S.A., Earth

December 1, 2016

I sat down to work out my schedule for the next week.

AHHHHH! NOOOO!

oops.
I might've spread myself a little thin.

December 2, 2016

Kyle and I repaired some cracks in our chimney.

... and there

Later on I tried to initiate sex.

Hey there.

watching TV while playing with his phone. The ultimate multitasker.

Somehow I ended up giving him a back rub instead.

... Hey... wait a second...

Knead Knead

December 3, 2016

I started an art only Instagram account, so I've been looking through old sketchbooks for fun pages to post.

Haha, I remember that!

I used to draw lots of overlapping images on the same page, sometimes with color.

its huge.

oh well

yawn.

December 4, 2016
Danny
Megan
Liz
Gilmore Girls
Vegetarian
Tom Yum Soup
DiDi

December 5, 2016
SNOW!
SNOW!
SNOW!

December 6, 2016

December 7, 2016

December 8, 2016

Megan and Danny came over to watch another new Gilmore Girls episode. We feasted on Taco Bell and gluten-free cookies.

My throat started feeling a little scratchy at the beginning of the night.

uh oh

December 9, 2016

Had probably the most productive day I've had in a while even though I'm sicker than I've been in years. Who'da thunk it?

SNIFFLE

December 10, 2016

December 11, 2016

Felt mostly better, so I went to Picnic, Portland's craft fair.

Did you have fun at your white person convention?

Yes, I did.

But being around that many people definitely reactivated my sore throat.

Lousy humans and their GERMS.

December 12, 2016

December 13, 2016

December 14, 2016

It's pretty awkward to have someone working on your house.

...Am I supposed to just stand here?

December 15, 2016

After I spent an hour cleaning the house...

sniff sniff

UH OH, ...it smells like cat puke.

...but where is it?

Kyle! You have to come see this! It's HILARIOUS!

December 16, 2016
SNRK
TOSS
FOOM

December 17, 2016

Kyle and I were supposed to go to Boston today, but a snowstorm kept us home.

I can't believe they haven't plowed our street yet.

December 18, 2016
Diagnosis: Birthday.

BIRTHDAY PRESENTS!
SOCKS
Homemade Simpsons DVDS
18
19
THE BOOK OF FROGS
BOOKS

Prognosis: Excellent.

December 19, 2016

*a sleeping bag hoodie

(we watched xmas horror films)

December 20, 2016
Fake tree
Real presents
When I was younger, I didn't like Christmas very much, but sometime in the last few years I started to get into it.
Maybe it's because of the hilarious wrapping paper.

December 21, 2016
I don't have many specific memories of events,
we used to have Thanksgiving together every year.
I know our families were close.
But I very vividly remember your house,
and a strong feeling of comfort and kindness that radiated from you.
In loving memory of Mary Ann Wells 1952-2016

December 22, 2016

I felt self-conscious in my new winter coat

It's not really cold enough to warrant this monstrosity.

I felt self-conscious at the bank.

Please don't comment on the amount of money I'm depositing.

I felt self-conscious everywhere.

What're YOU lookin' at?

December 23, 2016

December 24, 2016

I dreamed that I saw my dad in the crowd at a baseball game.

!

He was carrying a big, fluffy golden retriever.

I spent a long time searching for him to no avail.

When I finally caught up to him, he was getting into a dark brown '80s Toyota Tercel.

Our interaction was remarkably anti-climatic.

You've been ALIVE this whole time?!

Yeah, well, y'know

Yesterday was the 5-year anniversary of his death.

December 25, 2016

December 26, 2016

Today is my mom's birthday, a holiday far more important to me than Christmas.

(The most sacreligious infographic ever?)

In fact I've never celebrated Christmas with any religious intent.
I'm only in it for the stocking.

I really hate cleaning up after the holidays.

Now where am I supposed to put all this stuff?!

December 27, 2016
I've been thinking a lot about what productivity personally means to me.
Did I earn this nap?

Everyday I wake up excited to tackle the multiple projects I've got going.
I can draw my dailies.
Format some pages for my new comic collection.
work on book pitch.
emails.
write some Coady and The Creepies.

But my energy doesn't last very long. I'm usually exhausted by late morning.
...or maybe it's ok if I only get to one thing today?
YAWN

December 28, 2016

As this year nears its end I've been thinking a lot about what New Years means to me.

I'm not a fan of NYE from a celebratory perspective, it's more of a reminder of all the things I DIDN'T do this year.

It would be good to have a brain that focuses on the things I DID do.

Sorry toots, it's been 35 years. You're stuck with me.

But even I can't deny the allure of having the blank slate of a New Year to dust myself off and try again.

...Let's go exploring.

December 29, 2016

I guess I'm a little burnt out on these diary comics.

Another day spent doing nothing but drawing. What spin can I put on it this time...

I guess it's a good thing that next year I'm changing the scope of this patreon to encompass longer-form storytelling.

Blah, blah, blah, me, me, me.*

I'll probably miss this, tho.

And if I'm being honest, I'm afraid I'm biting off more than I can chew.

*longer comics will likely still be about me. Sorry.

December 30, 2016

I racked up a pretty decent score on the Addams Family pinball at Arcadia.

December 31, 2016
I have the craziest dating stories.
You should get someone to illustrate them and make a graphic novel.
That's actually my job: I make comics about my life.
Well, if you made a book of my stories I'd make you an AWARD-WINNING graphic novelist.
How do you know I'm not already an award-winning graphic novelist?
Yep, you'd win awards with me.

THANK YOU

Eternal gratitude to my patreon subscribers; these comics would not exist without your generous support.

And to every one else who encouraged me to document my life in 3 panels and put up with being characters in this book.

Y'all are the best!

Author biography

Liz Prince is the author of Will You Still Love Me If I Wet the Bed?, Alone Forever, Tomboy, and Be Your Own Backing Band. She also created the comic series Coady and the Creepies with artist Amanda Kirk.

Her hobbies include pinball, eating burritos, and looking at frogs. I'm assuming you read this book, so you know that shit already.

PUNK

Anyway, she's super awesome and you should be impressed. Check out more of her work at lizprincepower.com if you don't believe me!

PUNK

LOOK BACK AND LAUGH